Change,
Communication & Relationships
in the Catholic Church

Other books from the *Authortity and Governance Project*
published by Matthew James Publishing Ltd

Diocesan Dispositions and Parish Voices in the Roman Catholic Church
edited by Noel Timms

"You Aren't One of the Boys", Authority in the Catholic Priesthood Noel Timms

A Painful Process edited by Andrew Bebb and Anna Roper

Authority in Roman Catholicism Bernard Hoose

CHANGE, COMMUNICATION & RELATIONSHIPS IN THE CATHOLIC CHURCH

D G BARKER

Matthew James Publishing Ltd

First published 2002 by:

Matthew James Publishing Ltd
19 Wellington Close
Chelmsford, Essex CM1 2EE

ISBN 1 898366 74 8

Typeset in Bembo & Copperplate by Linda East
Cover design by Peter Robb
Printed in Great Britain by J W Arrowsmith, Bristol

CONTENTS

INTRODUCTION

CHANGE, COMMUNICATION AND RELATIONSHIPS

This booklet is concerned with the experience of change, communication and relationships in Catholic parishes. It is based upon twelve local case studies, supplemented by evidence from interviews with diocesan personnel. Six dioceses collaborated in preparing a series of diocesan and parish studies. These examine how bishops, with their advisors and key personnel, endeavour to make the best use of the scarce human and financial resources available to them; their vision, their plans, the way they go about God's work. They also explore the reality as it is experienced at parish level. About 100 senior diocesan personnel were interviewed including the six bishops. The twelve parishes were selected for special study by the bishops concerned. The bishops were asked to nominate parishes which had recently experienced a period of change or transition. The case studies involved interviews with some 350 parishioners and clergy in the selected parishes.

A majority, but not all, of those interviewed was active in parish work. They were generous spirited in their responses and frank in their opinions. In their frankness, these parishioners were critical about many aspects of the Church, its organisation and teaching. They did not seek to undermine the Church but, rather, to present the reality as they experienced it. The problems are in common ownership of all involved in the Church and, once identified, their solution is a shared responsibility. As Mgr. Peter Verity has said *"The natural desire of those involved in providing pastoral care is to try to smooth over the cracks, to pour oil on troubled waters, to pacify, to reassure and affirm people where they are... But true pastoral care means telling the truth rather than turning a blind eye to reality. It means being honest and open with people about the future and this will often be uncomfortable and challenging."* He also notes the favourable reaction that such truth telling evoked in his own diocese when the diocesan administrator prepared a pastoral letter setting out clearly and frankly the difficulties caused by the current shortage of priests. *"There was a sense of 'thank God someone is facing the reality of the situation and being honest with us about it'."*[1] The parish case studies are intended to be such an attempt at positive and constructive 'truth telling'.

Obviously, it is inappropriate to generalise about the Church in Great Britain on the basis of 350 interviews in twelve parishes. Nevertheless, there is great consistency of opinion among the diverse parishes surveyed. Important questions are raised and there are lessons to be learned. It is hoped that the

1

material presented will be of benefit to members of parish councils, pastoral planning teams and others concerned about the vitality and relevance of parish life to the challenge of the gospel. The research forms part of the Queen's Foundation *Authority & Governance* initiative, details of which are summarised in an appendix to the booklet. Reference to Queen's Foundation publications based on the research are indicated in bold type in the text which follows. A full list is contained in the appendix.

Part One: The Background

Social Change in Twentieth Century Britain

Human Life Transformed

All of us could produce our own list of the major events and developments in the twentieth century and what they meant for our families. We might think of the political upheavals, the collapse of Empire, the armed conflicts, the 'Cold War.' We might prefer to concentrate on the amazing developments in biology, medicine, technology and communications. Or, perhaps, focus upon education, employment, the struggle for justice and quality of life. The impact of these and other changes has fundamentally altered British society. The way people think, what they value and their social attitudes have changed – including attitudes to religion and the Church. Writing about one hundred years of social change since 1900, A H Halsey comments *"At the beginning of the century, Britain was still an imperial nation... the Union Flag flew over a fifth of the world's people and territory. At the end, its fluttering was confined to one hundredth of the worlds population... In fact, the whole structure of human life the world over has been transformed."*[2]

Britain had a population of 37 million in 1901. Birth and death rates were high. For three out of every four people in Britain, work meant manual labour. Most families existed at subsistence level. Two out of every five males aged 75 years or over were still working. Wealth was concentrated in a few hands. The richest 5% of the population owned 80% of the wealth. People married late and quite a high proportion of adults remained single. Married women stayed at home. Through a combination of social custom and "the moral surveillance of religion", divorce and illegitimate births were, Halsey reminds us, virtually non-existent and harshly punished. The country lost 2.4 million people through emigration between 1901-1931.

Between 1931-2001, Britain gained 3 million people from net immigration. By the end of the century, the population had grown to 57.5 million (an increase of 55% since 1900). Major cities became racially mixed. Birth, infant mortality and overall death rates fell. People began living much longer – with consequent implications for family life. In 1998, one in every six citizens was aged over sixty-five compared to one-in twenty in 1900. Households became much smaller and there was a big increase in the number of people living alone. More people were in education and employment than ever before. Hours of work fell. The percentage of economically active males in the workforce declined and only one in ten males aged over 65 years had a job. Paid holidays and foreign travel dramatically increased. Most workers were now in white collar jobs – a reflection of the country's changing industrial structure and the increasing proportion of working women.[3] Real income per head from economic activity increased four and a half times between 1900-1995. Wealth was also more equally distributed. By 1995 the share of the richest 5% had fallen to 25% of total wealth – though the trend to greater equality in wealth and income was actually reversed in the final decades of the century.

MIXED BLESSING

Despite the huge benefits, social changes were a mixed blessing as Halsey notes. "*Britain ended the century as a European leader of extra-marital and teenage births… divorce and cohabitation… in the first half of the century, domesticity was the norm for women after marriage. But especially since the early 1950's, the increasing participation of married women has been the most outstanding factor in the changing balance between employment and non-employment – a fact which raises many questions about the changing character of family life, and the relationship between marriage, kinship and economy in an advanced industrial society…*"[4] He also argues "*that all forms of traditional authoritative power faltered in the second half of the century – parents, politicians, priests and police as well as scoutmasters and schoolteachers all became less trusted and less popularly admired as the century wore on… the general net thrust of government over the century, aided by the two world wars, can be seen as being towards centralisation.*"[5]

The pattern of family life in Britain may be different now. The composition of the household may have changed. Yet, family preoccupations and quality of life remain of the utmost importance to the majority of people.[6] For example, most parents want their children to grow up well-mannered, unselfish, responsible and tolerant. Emphasis is also placed upon independence, autonomy and self-reliance. The high value given to family life is, nevertheless, accompanied by a growing unwillingness to tolerate unsatisfactory relationships. Partners see marriage, cohabitation and family life as opportunities for personal growth and self expression. People now demand openness in public institutions. They want a say in decisions which intimately affect their lives. They expect government, employers and, increasingly, the Church, to promote these values. But, as Halsey indicates, confidence in public institutions and the political process has diminished. Such dissatisfaction is linked to a rise in public protest and the assertion of 'rights'.[7]

Reviewing the evidence of studies of the moral and social condition of Europe (reported in the European Values Surveys) a decade ago, I suggested that *"The morally autonomous Europeans, disengaged from the churches, disenchanted with democratic institutions and the political process, demanding greater involvement in the decisions which affect their lives and willing to take direct political action to achieve their aims, pose a fundamental challenge to political and religious leaders. ...Leaders are an elderly and remote group whose messages do not resonate with the young. They are in danger of addressing only their shadows. Fundamental reform of political and religious structures and a revised notion of the obligations of citizenship may be necessary to reintegrate political, religious and community life in a way consistent with more egalitarian social relations."*[8] The new generation of political leaders may be younger, but, judging by events at the beginning of the new millennium, they are as, or more, out of touch with their constituents than in 1990.

As far as the Catholic Church is concerned, the attitudes described above do not sit easily with its claims to exercise sacred power and authority over lay people. Nor is there a younger generation of leaders in place. Yet, social change has had a profound influence on the Church.

THE CATHOLIC POPULATION

SOME FIGURES

There are about 4.7m adult Catholics in Great Britain (10% of the population)[9]. In the late seventies it was still possible to describe English Catholics as a "relatively young and working class community".[10] That is no longer the case. By the end of the century, the age, education and class structure of the Catholic Church was similar to the British population as a whole.[11] Sunday mass attendance has declined, falling by 50% since the mid-nineteen-fifties. About a quarter of British Catholics now attend mass once a week. Women, the elderly and those from the managerial and professional classes are more likely to attend mass than men, young people or manual workers. Married Catholics who regularly attend Sunday mass are almost certain to be married to another Christian.

FORTRESS CHURCH

In Britain, the Catholic Church of the first half of the twentieth century was very different from that which emerged in the second half. The Church of the first half of the century has been variously described as '*a fortress church*', '*an enclosed village*', '*as complete a life world as possible*', '*a subculture within wider society*'.[12] It was a defensive minority – both in relation to secular society and to other Christian denominations. Allegiance to the Pope, obedience to religious authority, a separate education system, strict moral norms, an emphasis on conducting social life within a Catholic context, marriage to a Catholic partner, a Latin liturgy and distinctive practices such as Friday abstinence and May processions all contributed to a specific Catholic identity and separateness. Desmond Ryan, in his study of parish life, argues that an important element in this Catholic identity was immaturity in adult religious life. Priests, he suggests, *"had the power over resources, over consciences, over education, over the common life of the community. They used that power to achieve what they thought the Catholic priesthood was there to achieve: identikit Catholics, pressed from a mould; pious, moral, docile, obedient – and passive. The ideal Catholic was the child."*[13] We are now reaping the harvest, he says, of seeds sown many years ago. Unused to it, most Catholics remain unwilling to accept responsibility in the parish. He suggests a number of reasons. An authoritarian Church did not train its priests to be good at human relations. Nor did it encourage lay people to use their gifts. Faith was reduced to dogma. Formulas governed behaviour. Obligations such as mass attendance were emphasised. Obedience rather than a free and mature response to the Gospel was the primary requirement.

DISSOLVED SUB-CULTURE

Not all Catholics were 'imprisoned' within the fortress. M P Hornsby-Smith urges us to be careful in assuming that *all* British Catholics were the same and that the *whole* Church *"up to the 1950's was a cohesive, tightly knit body, sharing the same values and beliefs, substantially united under a clerical leadership and manifesting an absence of divisive conflicts"*.[14] There was variety, he says, – of Catholic origins, social backgrounds and beliefs. A significant proportion of Catholics were immigrants, from Ireland, other parts of Europe and the Commonwealth. They differed in social class and culture from the old established 'recusant' British Catholic families who resisted clerical control. Importantly, the English working class, both agricultural labourers and urban industrial workers, had been largely indifferent to religion, – at least since the seventeenth century.

What is clear, he suggests, is that by the mid nineteen-eighties the distinctive Catholic sub-culture had *dissolved*. Catholics had become like everyone else. They were more open, and inclusive, more tolerant and less judgemental. Most Catholics now married non-Catholics. Those who did so were also more likely to be unorthodox in belief and practice. At the same time, he detected disaffection among young people with the 'institutional' Church and noted the emergent women's movement. He reported that the alienation of British working class people from the institutional Church was becoming more apparent. It had previously been disguised by large scale Irish immigration. He also warned of a growing gap, experienced by other Christian denominations, between those who were active and involved in the Church (usually educated, middle class and orthodox) and the "ordinary person in the pew".

Finally, Hornsby-Smith suggested that, as its members become more like the rest of the population, it would be more difficult for the Church to persuade them that *" there are specific goals for which it ought to strive and interests it ought to defend… If a sign of maturity is the emergence of independent judgement and responsible action, then one might judge that English Catholics, while they might quite happily be more ready than in previous years to 'make up their own minds' on religious and moral matters, are nevertheless too passive or lethargic to make a proportionate contribution to the political decision-making of British society."* Important exceptions to Hornsby-Smith's general point might be pro-life issues and the response to poverty, particularly in the third world. Also, as Catholics have become more integrated within wider society and less distinctive as a minority community, they have had opportunities to express their social and political convictions through secular channels. Indeed, evidence from the European Values Surveys shows that *"In all fields of activity, the more intimately people are involved in the institutional church, the more likely they are to be actively engaged as volunteers"* in working for the common good.[15] In fact, the majority of workers, both paid and unpaid, in UK voluntary organisations are Christian.

YOUNG CATHOLICS

GENERATIONAL CHANGE

Commenting upon generational differences in religious and social attitudes at the turn of the millennium, Alison Park of the National Centre for Social Research suggests that *"Nowhere is the gulf between old and young so dramatic as in their religious attachment."* She notes the growth in the unchurched throughout the eighties and nineties. Those aged 18-24 are now twice as likely as the over 55 age group to have no religious attachment. The evidence indicates she says that *"religious attachments seem to assert themselves at an early age* and then to persist. *People certainly do not seem to become more religious as they age. Moreover, although attitudes within each cohort are relatively stable, younger cohorts are consistently less religious than are older ones… as the older, more religious generations die out, they will probably give way to less religious generations, leading to an overall diminution of religious attachment in Britain.*" Similar differences exist in attitudes to sexual permissiveness. The 25-34 year olds are the most liberal in their views, though a majority of all age groups disapproves of extra-marital affairs. Significantly, approval of abortion – when the woman does not wish to have the child – has increased across all the generations within the past twenty years with a majority of those over seventy now in favour – *"what used to be unacceptable has simply become more normative among all generations as the practice of abortion has become widespread."*[16] Park's conclusions are echoed by Grace Davie in her study of religion in modern Europe. *"…Religious illiteracy is widespread in modern Europe amongst younger generations… it seems entirely possible that the religious memory of Europe – at least in its traditional form of a basic understanding of Christian teaching – might cease to exist, except as a branch of specialist knowledge; it is indeed precarious."* [17]

INDIVIDUAL CONSCIENCE HAS DISPLACED EXTERNAL AUTHORITY

Young Catholics have been influenced by these trends, but, perhaps not to the degree that one might first expect by their absence from Sunday Mass. Indeed, the Church *membership* of young Catholics appears to be holding up better than their peers in other Christian churches, though their *attendance* and *participation* rates are low. NOP report that in 1997 over one-third of 'adult' Catholics in England and Wales were aged 15-35 years – that is, much as would be expected from the number of young adults in the UK population. This compares with just over one-quarter of Anglicans and one-fifth of Methodists and Baptists who are in the same age group, a significant under-representation.[18]

In a small scale, qualitative, study of young Catholics with varying degrees of religious conviction, Fulton suggests that young 'core' Catholics are deeply committed but there are signs among some of the 'intermediate' group of 'superficiality'. He believes that young core Catholics in Britain are reformist in their desire for structural change, inculturation and mission in the Church. They retain a strong belief in the value of human life tempered with sympathy and respect for the choices made by others. Young Catholic women, though, may be more liberal than men in their attitudes to sex. The faith of young Catholics, he suggests, is not devotional or "sin centred" in the traditional sense.

"It may mean that young core Catholics are more content and less guilty than previous generations, but, it does not mean that they are less religious… we find religious and moral responses coming from within the subject rather than from without… Individual conscience has displaced external authority in the matter of social and personal ethics… personal experience itself is used to uncover norms of conduct. For young modern Catholics, morality has become internal first and external second… they will do what they feel is right and proper rather than what has been announced by the Pope."[19] Fulton's sample was not statistically representative. It was also limited primarily to middle class young people in the south east of England and thus lacked the perspective of working class Catholics who were difficult to identify. The conclusions cannot therefore be generalised to all young Catholics. They are, however, broadly consistent with the results of the present enquiry.

FELLOWSHIP AND SELF-DISCOVERY

Young people do not appear to be comfortable in the static formal structures of parish life, preferring, rather, the experience of fellowship and self discovery within more temporary communities. For example, Grace Davie points to the success of the world youth days (attracting 1 million young people to Paris in 1997), the gathering of up to six thousand 18-25 year olds in Taize each summer, the annual Protestant Kirchentag initiatives in Germany which attract 100,000 middle class young people for four days, with thousands of additional casual visitors, and the regular presence of young helpers to assist the disabled in pilgrimage centres such as Lourdes. Pilgrimage, she suggests is a metaphor for modern living. *"Life becomes a form of perpetual seeking, a virtual reality in which the boundaries always recede… the closer we get to our goals, the more we realise that the ultimate prize or certainty eludes us."* In years gone by, pilgrimages used to build upon parish life as a means of renewing and energising commitment, but they can become an alternative, especially for the young *"who enjoy the company and the emotional high of the pilgrimage experience, but for whom dogmatic teaching and regular practice have less and less appeal".*[20] A major difficulty with the latter approach is that the strength of religious commitment is closely related to involvement in an enduring community of faith.[21]

CATHOLIC PRIESTS

RE-IMAGINING PRIESTHOOD

The Church explicitly recognises the changed context in which priests now exercise their ministry. It states *"The priestly office… is now carried out in an entirely new situation which comes to light as a result of humankind's new needs and from the nature of modern civilisation."*[22] Indeed, Fr. John O'Brien believes that the traditional priestly role has become impossible. It is remarkable, he says, that priests have been able to meet the demands upon them for so long. He does not believe that their training is at all appropriate to their current responsibilities and maintains that they are ill equipped to manage their workloads. The present situation, he suggests, is demoralising and made worse by child abuse scandals and resignations.[23]

The Council of Trent 1545-63 was of great significance in establishing the present system for the training of priests and its legacy remains. Called to clarify Catholic dogma, correct abuses and impose discipline on the Church, the Council endeavoured to renew diocesan and parish life. Its 'crowning achievement' is recognised as the invention of seminaries. Previously the training of diocesan priests had been limited and haphazard.[24] The priest – after Trent – was to be a man set apart from his parishioners, celibate and saintly. Friendships were discouraged. But, as the historian Eamonn Duffy points out, the vision of priesthood formed at the Council of Trent is *"slowly collapsing under the joint pressures of theological and social change… As society changes, as the Church calls on all the laity to claim and exercise their priesthood, and as we discover that the charisms which form the life of the Church are given to all and not just the clergy, we are confronted with an urgent need to re-imagine the ordained priesthood as the counter reformation re-imagined it and reinvented it."* [25]

There are 6500 Catholic priests in Britain. A little over three-quarters of them are diocesan priests, the remainder are members of religious institutes. Vocations to the priesthood have declined by 60% in the past thirty-five years and the number of priests dropped by one-fifth between 1980-1999. Consequently, the average age is now over sixty and at least a quarter are retired from active ministry. Many were formed for and committed to a model of ministry that is passing away. They are not at an ideal age to adapt to and embrace new approaches – though many are said to be more enthusiastic than younger, newly ordained priests. It is not surprising therefore to encounter a sense of loss at the passing of the old order and resistance to change.

NOT ONE OF THE BOYS

Noel Timms in *You Aren't One of the Boys* concludes that it is possible to classify priests into three broad groups each linked to a particular view of the Church. *"Priesthood can be seen as sacred, as functional and as communitarian. The*

Church can be seen as closed, as primarily an organisation or a developing mission."[26] He defines those in the first category as **'sacred priests in a closed Church'**. They perceive themselves as called, set aside, uniquely sharing Christ's ministry, possessing sacred authority as a direct channel of God or of salvation to the people. They tend to emphasise loyalty, divinely delegated clerical decision-making power, the unchangeability of Church teaching and clear boundaries to membership. The second group he defines as **'functionaries in an organisational Church'**. Such priests see the nature of priesthood as developing over time; not superior to the lay state but different. They feel an obligation to live out the promises made at ordination and to teach whatever the Church authorities require to be taught at the time. They seek to serve the Church by responding to needs as they arise and by implementing pastoral policy. Change is accepted if that is what the Church demands. They do not fear loyal dissent. They take account of individual motives for disagreement and the status of the teaching which is under discussion. The third category Timms refers to as **'communitarian priests in an open Church'**. Such priests do not see themselves as 'set apart' at all. They regard themselves as just "ordinary people with ordinary lives" working alongside others to build up the community and help parishioners exercise their common priesthood. The boundary with lay Catholics is blurred. They favour lay involvement in the appointment of priests. They regard their official functions as residual and their tasks as practical. They favour open discussion of the controversial issues facing the Church in the interests of future development, including: clerical celibacy; admission of the divorced and remarried to communion; inter-communion and Anglican orders.

EXORCISING THE GHOST

The three groups will adapt to change differently. Priests in the first category will clearly find it difficult. It is interesting to note that in the interviews conducted at diocesan level for **Diocesan Dispositions and Parish Voices**[27] priests reported three sets of attitudes to collaborative ministry. One group, perhaps between one third and one half of the priests in a diocese, favour collaboration with lay people. A second group are open to the idea – if not wholly convinced – but do not know how to go about it. They may also be concerned at the possibility of unrepresentative minorities of lay people exercising too much influence. A third group, perhaps between one-quarter and two-fifths, favour a more authoritarian mode of ministry and are opposed to collaboration. But, as Ryan has pointed out, *"As more priests try to build the* relationships upon which ministries and enablement depend, they find that the ghost of the old model of priesthood needs exorcising no less than the old model of parish."[28] Indeed, the late Fr. Norman Cooper maintained that "many clergy, though willing to sacrifice their status, lack the vision and skills to initiate collaboration with their lay colleagues... and... to engage effectively in group process that forms the foundation for collaborative ministry". Similar concerns might equally be expressed about the laity. For, as Fr. Cooper pointed out, such processes require self-awareness, emotional honesty and a willingness to deal with conflict in a mature way.[29]

THE INSTITUTIONAL CONTEXT

NO HIGHER FORM OF MINISTRY

In his contribution to **Governance and Authority in the Catholic Church,** Fr. David McLoughlin points out that in 'Lumen Gentium' the Dogmatic Constitution of the Church, "The Second Vatican Council defined the Church as primarily a local entity gathered round its bishop... the universal Church was presented as the network of local churches. There is no higher form of ministry in the Church than that of the local bishop... the bishop's call comes from God... rather than the bishop of Rome... with each bishop responsible both for the unity of the local church and carrying a shared responsibility for the unity of the world Church."[30] The bishop is seen as immersed in, listening to, nourished by and reflecting back to his community what he has received from the witness of the faith lived locally. The American bishop, Matthew Clark emphasises that such listening involves the weak and marginalised as well as the strong and noble, to enable each bishop to "testify before the Great Church to the faith and practice of his own particular church".[31]

There are considerable practical difficulties which limit the effectiveness of the bishop's role in the local church. Dioceses are geographically too large and complex for the vision of Vatican II to be effective. Parishioners have little or no sense of active engagement with their diocese. Many bishops do not, therefore, have the necessary rich and intimate relationships with their church members.

Importantly, the authority of bishops has been eroded. First, it has been worn down by social change. Second, it has been undermined by increasing centralisation in the Church – driven by a more juridical and hierarchical (pre-Vatican II) model of church governance which stresses the authority of the Universal Church and the primacy of the pope.

DANGEROUS FOR THE LOCAL LIFE OF THE CHURCHES

Many of the characteristics of the modern papacy, including control of the appointment of bishops, have their origin neither in scripture nor in the writings of the early Fathers of the Church. Eamonn Duffy suggests, rather, that these powers are quite recent. They are the result of historical accident and confusion. *"For the first time, the Church has a papacy whose power is almost equal to its claims. This is certainly dangerous for the local life of the churches…"*. One of the consequences is that the significant increase in the centralisation of power and authority which Halsey notes in secular government during the twentieth century has been paralleled in the Church – particularly since the publication of the 1917 code of canon law. The danger, as another historian Robert Markus has pointed out, is the arbitrary and possibly unjust use of that power, which undermines the authority of the local church. Duffy is nevertheless optimistic that *"what comes by historical accident may go by historical accident. The present powers of the popes in such matters as episcopal appointments are open to assessment on grounds of utility, efficiency and theological fitness, and might be changed on any one of these counts."*[32]

The issue of the legitimate authority of the local bishop has been taken up by – among others – Bishop Walter Kasper (now Cardinal President of the Pontifical Council for Christian Unity) and Archbishop John Quinn, the former President of the Bishops' Conference in the USA. Bishop Kasper argues that the Catholic tradition grants the local bishop, as Christ's delegate, the *"vital space"* to respond to the pastoral needs of his people in ways which go beyond papal norms.[33]

Archbishop Quinn has published a response to Pope John Paul II's call for dialogue about ways of exercising the papacy which are faithful to the mission of the Church but *"open to a new situation"*. He points to the positive role of constructive criticism throughout the history of the Church and comments:

"The question of centralization is encountered at the theological level in the doctrine of collegiality and communion. Theologically there seems to be a contradiction in the… growing centralisation on the part of Rome… and the teaching of the Church about collegiality and communion… At the practical level, centralization to the degree that it now exists presents a growing and impossible task in a world Church of such diversity and in an age of instant communication and rapid change…in the practical realm, it can decentralize, encourage diversity, elicit participation and implement the principle of subsidiarity and the doctrine of effective collegiality without running the risk of chaos…

"If the curia does not change, and decentralization does not take place, there will ensue great disorder in the Church because of its inability to respond to changing

situations with sufficient rapidity, and the inability of an omnicompetent central bureaucracy to have an adequate grasp of swiftly changing, multicultural situations.'[34]

The above issues are discussed in more detail in Bernard Hoose's booklet in this series **Authority in Roman Catholicism.**[35]

THE LOCAL CHURCH IN BRITAIN

A BEWILDERING ARRAY OF FINANCIAL PROBLEMS

It is in the above institutional context that our bishops exercise their responsibilities. There are thirty dioceses or 'Local Churches' in Great Britain, supporting some 3300 parish churches. As is well known, they are organised into two separate Bishops' Conferences; one for Scotland, the other for England and Wales. In **Diocesan Dispositions and Parish Voices,** Philip Grindell estimates that the total value, or net worth of the thirty dioceses is about £2.3 billion. He suggests that this is a conservative estimate because he feels he has probably underestimated the value of diocesan land, works of art and other treasures. The figures are based upon published diocesan accounts. These are difficult to read and interpret. The dioceses differ in the way they implement government accounting regulations. There are also slight differences in the accounting requirements for Scotland. The overall estimate takes no account of any separate diocesan trusts, the seminaries (at home and abroad) or other Church organisations. Importantly, the estimates also exclude the religious orders who maintain their own accounts. The £2.3 billion, therefore, is not intended to be a measure of the net worth of the whole institutional Church in Britain.[36]

At first glance, the sums involved look substantial. When divided between the parishes, or calculated as an amount per head of the Catholic population, however, they look modest. In fact, Grindell suggests that only two of the six dioceses he examined have the capacity to expand their activities. His figures also reveal that there are significant differences in wealth between the dioceses. In the six he studied, one has just 8% of all the mass attenders in the group, but, holds 22% of the total liquid assets (including investment properties, portfolio investments and net current assets). There are similarly wide variations in income and expenditure and in reserves. Among these six local churches, the diocesan *income surplus* per mass attender varies between £4-£157, and the diocesan *reserves* per mass attender range from £540-£2198 per head. These sums are important as they provide an indication of the ability of a diocese to meet the considerable financial demands which will be made upon it in the coming years.

Reserves may be modest, but, they are better than a decade ago. Commenting upon the figures, Grindell notes that "*Many dioceses appear to have entered the 1990's in financial difficulties but, generally, dioceses have emerged from the decade either in positions of relative strength, or, at least, with their finances under control.*" This has been achieved as a result of improved financial discipline – stimulated by the 1992-3 Charities Acts, bulk purchase schemes, sales of surplus properties, professionally guided investment management and a generous response from parishioners to appeals for funds. As in the commercial world, however, the cost of compliance with government legislation is high and rising. Diocesan incomes have remained buoyant despite falling parish congregations, but the situation is not sustainable. Parishioners are ageing and many are of pensionable age.

As far as expenditure priorities are concerned, he suggests that it is difficult to escape the conclusion that "*financial thinking in the dioceses is dominated by clergy matters, repairing buildings, running schools and paying ever more in salaries. Building repair and construction costs have been put on hold for a while in some cases but this seems to have done little to aid the expansion of pastoral activities.*" Dioceses he says, face a bewildering array of financial problems. Priests and congregations are ageing and declining. The human resource costs are increasing. It is necessary to provide for sick and elderly clergy and to meet the salaries of lay pastoral workers to replace them. Many dioceses have yet to prepare local parishes to meet the inevitable burden. The cost of maintenance and repair of buildings is rising, particularly for dioceses with a high proportion of listed, redundant or non-viable sites. Most importantly, there is concern about the low priority given to youth ministry and to the adult religious education initiatives necessary to revitalise the parishes and provide for their long term pastoral needs. Such initiatives would include joint formation with priests for collaborative work.

Lack of a well-developed and coherent pastoral strategy clearly inhibits financial planning. Part of the difficulty is the absence, at the most senior level, in many dioceses of specialist competence in pastoral strategy to match that which has been recruited from among the professionals in finance, education and social care. Planning for the emerging shortage of priests is not well advanced. Indeed, the diocesan studies raise serious questions about the extent to which the bishops engage in strategic planning at all. As Gerard Mannion the author of one of the reports phrased it "*That the diocese is so clearly lacking an articulated, well defined vision and forward planning is both a symptom and a further cause of how resources (particularly in terms of personnel) are at breaking point in a diocese which appears to think it is coping quite well."*

THE STIMULUS FOR CHANGE

The main stimulus for change at diocesan level in the past decade has not been primarily theological or pastoral, but rather the demands of the UK civil authorities. Government reform of Charity Law, educational reforms and social policy development, including child protection legislation have compelled the diocesan authorities to introduce changes. Strategic thinking appears to have lagged behind. The situation is complicated by tension between the requirements of canon law and the responsibilities imposed by the civil law. This can lead to duplication of structures and confusion of roles which diminishes pastoral effectiveness. Philip Grindell notes the call in one diocese for clarification and co-ordination of structural inter-relationships in the interests of coherent and effective management.

The bishops face formidable management problems. Some of these are related to the structure of the Church itself, some appear to be – in part at least – of their own making. Most point to the need for more informed and sensitive human-resource management.

- First, as the parish studies clearly demonstrate, there is no genuine sense of belonging to a 'local church' beyond the parish. Dioceses lack a coherent identity. In addition to geographical constraints, each diocese consists of distinct regional sub-cultures; rural and urban, rich and poor, indigenous and immigrant.

- Second, there are inconsistencies in the way senior diocesan appointments are handled. These appear to be related not so much to the size or complexity of the diocese itself but, rather, to the management style of the bishop. In particular they depend upon his attitude to delegation of power and responsibility, to compliance with the law and to reform of diocesan structures.

- Third, communication is actually poor, despite sometimes quite elaborate structures for consultation. Philip Grindell reports that some committees and commissions continue to exist which have outlived their usefulness and *"yet, take up the valuable time of hardworked clergy and laity"*. The result is uncertainty about how decisions are made and ignorance of diocesan plans and priorities. Some bishops actually find it difficult to take tough decisions. In a report on one diocese, I concluded that *"The bishop is not seen as relishing the role of decision-maker… in his concern to seek consensus, to avoid asking out of obedience, that which others find unacceptable, or to achieve the best outcome, he is said to hold back on decisions in the hope that a better option will emerge… Decision making is thus… 'problematic'… there is a lack of clarity about… priorities and a sense that decisions are made piecemeal"*. One serious consequence of poor communication emerging from the parish studies, is the sense of isolation and abandonment felt by parishes experiencing crisis. Examples will be given in Part II.

- Fourth, as has been noted, priests have very different notions of the nature of their ministry. As a result, both collaborative/participative and traditional/patriarchal models of authority co-exist among priests within the same diocese and even within the same parish. Some priests demand vision and direction from their bishop, but reject the strategic planning that should accompany it. Others prefer a 'laissez -faire' approach. Referring to his parishioners, one priest said *"As far as they are concerned, I'm the pope!"* Some like to work in isolation from their colleagues. *"I wouldn't like to share with other priests, I don't need that support,"* said one parish priest. All these factors have profound implications for parish life. Not least among them, is the fact that, short of priests and lacking the intimate connection with his people that the theology of the Local Church demands, the bishop may make inappropriate and insensitive appointments.

- Finally, lay staff in pastoral roles, especially women, experience a lack of awareness of, interest in, support for and professional supervision of their work which would be common practice in comparable secular occupations. Thus, Anna Rowland, reporting on conversations with female chaplains in Catholic schools and women engaged in lay ministries comments *"In only one case was the diocese seen as being actually supportive… It is the lack of interest in and awareness of the role shown by the diocese that was frequently commented upon… it is clear that supervision is being seen as important, but that it remains largely the initiative of the lay minister as opposed to the employer… those working in 'secular' institutions mainly schools and colleges were appraised and reviewed…in the same way as other staff… [but] those working in diocesan offices and parishes were more often without a system for appraisal and review."* Opportunities were available for staff to attend conferences and network with colleagues in similar situations. But, *"The lack of support, awareness and interest in what work was being done and by whom seemed to be a cause of genuine sadness and pain for many… this sadness remains unrecognised by many of those in the Church and particularly by the diocese."*[37] Rowland reminds us of Cardinal Hume's cautionary remark that the devotion and faithfulness of women have been taken for granted for too long and that warning signs should be heeded before it is too late. Nevertheless, she notes that a *"sense of vision and hope"* pervaded her interviewees responses and that their missionary commitment remained undiminished by management failures.

Louise Fitzgerald addresses the problems of change and development in the Church in **Diocesan Dispositions and Parish Voices.**[38]

Part Two: The 12 Parishes

Parish Life

Social and Pastoral Diversity

The total Catholic population in the twelve parishes studied (practising and non-practising) varied between 250-4500. Mass attendance rates ranged from 15%-60% of the estimated Catholic population. The highest rate was recorded in what had been, until the recent past, a tightly knit Catholic industrial village community.

The parishes which took part in the study were diverse. They included relatively privileged, white, educated middle class suburban localities, lower middle class neighbourhoods and urban parishes experiencing unemployment, crime, ethnic tension and violence. There were small geographically dispersed rural communities and demoralised industrial villages. Some had stable populations. Others experienced seasonal variations or high turnover of mass attenders – for example due to tourism or shifting military personnel at a nearby base. Some exhibited a strong local Catholic identity, in others there were still vestiges of historical anti-Catholic sentiment.

The changes experienced were similarly diverse. Two parishes appeared very stable, with little evident disruption. In other cases, parish life had been completely transformed by economic and social change. A number of parishes were in areas adjusting to the decline or disappearance of traditional industries. Several had been affected either by slum clearance or loss of population. In one ethnically mixed and very disadvantaged parish, two-thirds of the mass attenders came from outside the parish boundaries. Social inclusion and community building, particularly among local disaffected young black people, presented a real challenge. Some parishes were coping with the results of urban development. Several were in localities affected by both the decline of a traditional industry and the creation of a new town or major housing programme. The older residents in formerly tightly knit industrial communities which had ceased to be viable were rather demoralised. Some of these were adapting to the influx of 'incomers' to new housing developments. It made it difficult for them to respond positively to parish reorganisation. Shortage of priests and falling congregations led to pastoral reorganisation in other parishes. Several had been merged or 'clustered' with neighbouring parishes. Religious sisters might have joint responsibility for pastoral care and administration in such circumstances. There were problems of acceptability, of sharing a parish priest, of trying to build a Christian community among people who differed in their social backgrounds, interests and desire to mix. As will be seen, there was also trauma and change caused by abuse and behavioural problems among some clergy. The latter difficulties were made worse by diocesan mismanagement. All of these elements need to be borne in mind when considering the relatively low levels of participation reported in many of the parishes studied. They make inevitable demands upon people's personal and family priorities and their emotional and physical energy.

SIGNIFICANT CONSENSUS: IS THIS AS GOOD AS IT GETS?

The parishes included in the study were chosen by their diocesan bishop. He was asked to identify parishes that had been through a time of change or transition. The research team thought that this would help parishioners to discuss important issues still fresh in their minds. Commenting on the selection, M P Hornsby-Smith notes *"The parishes were located in the north, south, east and west and included both urban and rural and inner city and working class parishes... While no claims are made that the parishes are statistically representative of all the parishes in Scotland and England, it is clear that between them they cover a very wide variety of circumstances and experiences."*[39]

All of those interviewed were selected by the parish clergy after consultation with the interviewers. Three hundred and fifty women and men were involved. They included young and old, but, the majority were middle aged. Most were active in the parishes studied. Their wide ranging roles encompassed most aspects of parish life. These included administrative duties (parish councils, finance and planning teams, neighbourhood co-ordination groups), youthwork and social activities, pastoral and liturgical responsibilities (catechists, eucharistic ministers, readers, musicians). Such people tend to be among the most orthodox and committed of Catholics.[40] They cannot be dismissed as disaffected or ill informed about the realities of parish life. Their opinions indicate a high degree of consistency across the country and in different kinds of parish. Though frequently quite critical, their views were almost always offered in a spirit of generosity, goodwill and humour – and should be interpreted in that spirit. They were intended to be constructive and from 'within the family'. As one respondent put it *"It's just the same as for adult children. They can say 'I love my mum and dad, but, they don't half talk twaddle sometimes,' that's no reason to leave the family."*

The parish clergy were also interviewed and their opinions have been taken into account in what follows. Many of the parish priests selected were exceptional men – competent, caring and spiritual. Half of them held diocesan appointments in addition to their parish responsibilities. Parishioners recognised their good fortune. Some expressed concern about what would happen if the parish priest was moved. The quality of the priests was no doubt a factor influencing the bishops' choice of parishes to participate in the enquiry. But, the combination of exceptional priests and committed lay Catholics in the parishes studied prompts the question *"Is this as good as it gets?"*

The material which follows is based upon the research reports which were prepared for each of the twelve participating parishes, supplemented by direct quotations from the parishioners themselves and occasional references to third parties. These quotes are italicised. Very occasionally, it has been necessary to alter the wording of a direct quotation to protect the anonymity of a priest or a bishop, but, the meaning has always been preserved. Quotations from the research reports are not italicised.

CHANGE IN THE PARISH: AUTHORITY & ATTITUDES TO ROME

A FEELING FOR GOD

The twelve parish studies reveal a great deal of personal commitment to the Catholic faith and goodwill towards the Church. But they also reveal uncertainty, pain and frustration. They suggest that the majority of active Catholics value the Mass and cherish the Eucharist. They hold the Pope in personal esteem. They are, typically, supportive of their bishop, some regarding him with quiet affection. They are loyal to their priests, even in difficult circumstances. Most, but not all, appreciate the greater openness and more relaxed atmosphere of parish life since Vatican II. Some are fortunate to enjoy good – even warm – personal relationships with able, sensitive, and prayerful pastors. Yet, at the same time – as one of the parish reports described the situation – the involvement of Catholics with their parishes has become more fragile in recent years.

People are said to *"retain a feeling for God rather than an allegiance to the Church."* This is particularly true of younger parishioners. Catholic life – social and religious – no longer revolves around the Church. Consequently, people more easily withdraw from parish life than thirty years ago or, sadly, are driven away. Falling church attendances bear witness to the size of the problem. The reason for lapsation may be as simple as a change of address, a temporary practical difficulty or family circumstance involving short term non–attendance which becomes permanent. For some, embarrassment or low self–esteem resulting from unemployment or marital breakdown leads to disengagement. For others, the cause may be apparently rigid, insensitive teaching which is not consistent with conscience or experience, *"nobody openly made you feel bad, but, the teachings and readings put you off"*. It may be an inappropriate pastoral response to a specific problem. It may be a lack of humanity, a failure to treat the lay person with dignity, courtesy and respect. It may be an inability or unwillingness to acknowledge the fullness of the lay baptismal vocation – female and male. For some it may be indifference. There are clearly important challenges to be faced – but none are insurmountable with optimism, hope and a willingness to face the reality of the situation. This is what parishioners in the Queen's study have attempted to do.

There is widespread agreement about the changes which have taken place in the Church over the past thirty years. Social trends have profoundly influenced attitudes to the authority of the bishops and to Church teaching. They have also affected the relationship of ordinary Catholics with their local parish. *"People come when they feel they need us and go away again"* said one parish priest. Active Catholics distinguish between the Church as they experience it within the parish on the one hand, and as they perceive it at the institutional level in Rome on the other. They also distinguish between membership of a universal Church of fellow Christians – about which most are positive – and the jurisdiction of the Church authorities – about which most are not.

Many (including priests interviewed) are open to the possibility of optional celibacy and married priests. The practical difficulties are recognised. For some, they are too big a hurdle. For others, they are seen as common to other professions such as medicine. A significant minority also favour the ordination of women. *"…there is a lost generation of new parish priests because of celibacy"*, *"People know that married priests and women priests will happen."*, *"Let priests marry. Yes to women priests – very much… As long as the word of God is being preached"*. General absolution was proposed as a response to the decline in personal confession. It was well received in parishes where it had been experienced; *"it took a great hold."* One young man said that he found confession *"nerve-racking; a chore not a privilege. General absolution is more comfortable."* Priests, though, continue to set great store by the benefits of individual confession and may not favour General Absolution as an alternative.

People continue to feel a connection to the Pope and with Rome *"It is still important to us. People still pay attention to things said in Rome. Being a Catholic you still listen."* For some it is a reminder of the old certainties, *"The Pope is the last bastion."* *"He's old fashioned, an excellent Pope, good for the Church."* Sadly, for the majority of Catholics, the connection is weakening and is being undermined because Rome is perceived as remote, out of touch with and unsympathetic towards the experiences of ordinary people.

Many Catholics sense that a good number of their priests agree with them and that their bishops have problems of their own with Rome. One parish priest commented *"The clergy see that you can't have a loyal opposition today."* The authorities are seen as frequently insensitive (especially to women) and unrealistic in their claims. *"I worry about the rigidity of Rome... The Curia is out of touch with reality and the people... particularly the pressures of family and life".* People are convinced that Rome does not listen. Consequently, it may be dismissed as largely irrelevant to their daily lives. *"We now take our own decisions despite the Vatican"* *"We are not bothered about what comes from Rome. They are detached from reality."* There is, as one of the parish reports phrased it, "a significant estrangement from official teaching." Particular teachings are said to put an 'intolerable strain' upon obedience.

The more closely the teaching impacts upon people's intimate personal lives, the greater the likelihood of rejection if it conflicts with experience. Examples include contraception, divorce and the role of women in the Church. Referring to divorce and remarriage, one parish priest commented *"There is lots of inconsistency and strong feeling. People feel they are doing their best and see themselves as victims rather than sinners."* Another priest said that teaching should not be *"laid out like a blanket... People must apply a truth to the core... each situation must be treated on its merits".* The head of a Catholic primary school worried about the effect on Catholic children of the exclusion of their parents from the sacraments. A quarter of her pupils came from homes in which parents were divorced. What, she asked, was the church teaching them about the unforgivable sinfulness of their parents?

I DON'T KNOW WHAT THE CHURCH TEACHES

There is also, it has to be said, much ignorance about – and no great interest to discover – the details of Church teaching. Part of the confusion is created by priests themselves. Succeeding parish priests may hold differing theological viewpoints. Some priests may filter out teachings with which they disagree. Lay people readily acknowledge their ignorance. *"I don't know what the Church actually teaches about a whole range of issues and I have been involved with it for many years."* The little that filters through is frequently controversial and mediated mainly via the press. Regrettably, the Catholic press does not appear to enjoy a high reputation, they *"are not exactly visionary"*. Even if people did know more, some say *"it wouldn't make much difference"*, *"people are no longer interested in the 'nitty gritty' of Church teaching"*.

There are a number of reasons for ignorance. Poor communications, unhelpful language and the style of presentation are among them. *"The message delivered from Rome can be communicated in very different ways. The Church needs good PR."* Another reason is said to be an outmoded structure. *" Look at the structure; his Holiness and all the different levels. At grass roots we are struggling. Even the biggest corporations have seen the need to get rid of all the layers... The Roman Catholic Church must look at greater participation."* One respondent works for a large international corporation with an open culture. The company encourages its employees to believe they have a genuine contribution to make, to share good ideas and take responsibility. He contrasted his company to the Church, which, he felt, had much to learn about the motivation and involvement of its members.

FLEXIBLE RULES AND PERUVIAN INDIANS

Most Catholics continue to feel part of the universal Church and many welcome the *"sense of history, continuity and belonging"* which comes from being *"part of a world-wide connection"* with other Catholic Christians, *"people who have the same moral standards as you."* Some regard the universal dimension of the Church as more significant than a relationship with the diocese *"Universality is the hallmark of Catholicism. Catholics have an inbred sense of universality which by-passes the diocese."* Indeed, a minority wish to emphasise their 'Roman' Catholicism – *"The Pope is there to keep us on the straight and narrow"*, *"We feel near the Pope but I don't feel part of a united Church"*. *"The bishop should do what the Pope says."* But, the connection is weakening. Many now reject the universal jurisdiction of the Roman authorities.

The Church, one respondent noted, harking back to the days of the fortress Church in which older parishioners were raised, *"used to be the whole of people's lives, now it's on the edges"* and according to another *"Rules have to be flexible – they may not apply to Peruvian Indians!"* There is anxiety among a minority that those in authority appear more intent upon maintaining the institution than preaching the Gospel. Despite the personal esteem in which he is held, many people are also concerned about the age and frailty of the Pope and of others with major responsibility – *"You hear 'the Pope says' and you just switch off"*, *"The Pope is not in a fit condition to rule and the Cardinals are not either"*, *" Most people feel that there should be a much younger Pope. What age is he now? He must be getting senile… My own family think the Pope is past it. They don't think he is infallible."* One young man commented *"I don't have a clue what the Pope says or does. He is so old. He is unable to communicate with people. If the Pope is supposed to govern, you should have someone who is able to communicate his opinions. He is not front page news. I don't get hold of his opinions."*

FREELY OUT OF NEED

Thankfully, the parish is experienced as less authoritarian, more open and relaxed, more loving, more tolerant and more flexible than in years gone by. *"People today come to mass more freely out of need and love of God"*. Indeed, one reason advanced for low current practice rates is that people remain unaware that the Church has changed. Parishioners are open to a guiding role for the Church. It is the quality, authenticity and manner of exercising authority that is important. Priests, however, can no longer expect to exercise authority by virtue of their office. Respect has to be earned. They are no longer the dominant voice in the community. They have to offer convincing reasons for what they teach and demand. One curate welcomed the development. He could not, he said, *" be an agent for a pre-digested, dogmatic, oversimplified account of the gospel that leaves no room for the Holy Spirit and no room for an individual response"*.

People appreciate the fact that priests tend to be more approachable, more 'down to earth' these days. Such priests *"reinforce the warmth, welcome and sense of community"* in the parish. They are seen, in the words of one report "as ordinary people with the same struggles, doubts and inadequacies as everyone else". Concern was, nevertheless expressed about the reluctance of priests to share power with lay people, especially women. The conservative attitudes of some seminarians and newly ordained priests was also remarked upon with concern. *" Curates are now of a traditional mind… whereas before we had mature men with experience and learning which brought something different, young curates bring the Pope and Rome into every service and pretext"*. One report commented that they "do not seem to be either the best adjusted or the most able". The attitudes of these young priests sit uneasily with those of their own generation reported in Part One.

An Informed Conscience?

Parishioners are described as better educated, more confident, more discriminating and more critical in their reception of church teaching than in previous generations. They are no longer susceptible to what one described as the '*brainwashing*' that was commonplace when people were fearful, in awe of the priest and lacking in understanding. The majority relate teaching to the pressures of contemporary life. As mentioned above, they are unwilling to assent to regulations that are in conflict with their conscience and experience. *"It may be what the Church says, but, it is not necessarily the Gospel."* People are sympathetic to those who, through poverty or circumstance, are unable to uphold the teaching of the Church. Many respondents, young and old, expressed their support for the participation of the divorced in the sacraments. *"Here there's lots of support for divorcees, with only a minority against."* They advocate forgiveness and inclusion, looking at divorced people with *"Jesus eye"*, especially victims of domestic violence.

One challenging implication of the tendency towards greater autonomy in moral and spiritual life is a need to look closely at oneself from a spiritual point of view and discern the will of God. *"Until the sixties people were used to being told what was right or wrong. They were told and that was it. Some look back with nostalgia. People are now being challenged to look at their own morality. They are going through trauma. The Church may lose some of its moral authority, but, qualitatively the moral authority of the 'People of God' will increase."* Views differed on the extent to which parishioners are willing to engage in such soul searching. A number of the reports were not optimistic. The appetite for 'faith development' was limited. As one respondent put it *"today we need to go with our own conscience – but is our conscience right? An informed conscience is not sought."*

The Elderly And The Reprehensible Middle-Aged

The elderly are generally seen by others as most resistant to – and least comfortable with – change. Out of loyalty and obedience, they are regarded as more likely than younger age groups to abide by rules with which they disagree. Some are said to be disillusioned at the sweeping away of traditional piety and practice – *"where have the ten commandments gone?"* Some are believed to have fallen away *"disappointed because of revelations of abuse"* and because of the declining numbers of priests. In the words of two reports, the elderly 'miss the mystique of the Church in which they were brought up', and 'look back with a sense of loss to the old days and the sense of spiritual and social solidarity which attended the regular discharge of religious obligations'. Others, apparently, worry about the weakening moral stance of the Church.

The picture emerging from the elderly themselves is more complicated. One ninety year old was quoted as an example of an elderly person with an openness to change. Some elderly respondents questioned teachings on divorce and clerical celibacy. Others wondered why abortion was 'forgivable' but not divorce and remarriage. Some said that they had always made up their own minds, but, kept their own counsel. One retired lady commented as follows:

"My generation recognised the authority of the Church and deferred to the rules…The Church is losing a lot of young people. Friends with the same background as me, brought up their children to believe in the rules. Yet they left… they say "It is a load of rubbish". Even friends of my own generation have left: problems through marriage; contraception is a big issue; the position of women. Strong women… felt the Church was a male dominated society. For the young it is the general authority thing, but is that just their age? When they have children will they need the example of the Church?…School is very important. Without Catholic primaries we would have fewer Catholics. People do not respect the Church as much as when I was a child… A lot of social life was through the Church…There was more social distance between priests and people. It is good that people now feel they can speak to priests if they have trouble. Women tend to accept authority a bit easier than men"

Middle-aged Catholics are perceived to question the authority of the Church and, increasingly, to exercise choice. They experience greater religious freedom, but, their critical attitudes are said to inhibit involvement with the Church. Some have disengaged due to a sense of sin because they could not accept Church teaching. Elderly people were said to regard such behaviour as more reprehensible than the conduct of young people. One middle aged lady offered the following assessment of changes in the Church over the past thirty years:

"The majority do not recognise the authority of the Church. The directive on contraception is not upheld, you can see that reflected in the number of children people have. It is not a secret if people have a vasectomy… People pick and choose from Rome's directives. They are challenging. You have to look at yourself, God's will and so on. Some people don't want to do that… When the Pope is speaking about public issues, more people are in agreement with him than on religious issues… Catholics don't feel a great connection with what is going on in Rome. When you are interested in something you have to seek it out… There has been a change in attitudes in the last thirty years… People don't want someone telling them what to do. They are more emancipated. The hierarchy was dictatorial

traditionally. It still is but much milder. There are genuine attempts to try and include lay people, women, ordinary people and the marginalised in decision-making. We are a pleasure seeking society… I believe the Church is right in trying to get people to live by Gospel values. I don't know that you can tell people what to do. You can't tell the poor what to do when they can't feed their families. Personally, I think more of the Papal documents than the diocesan, I try to get hold of them"

NOT COOL!

The young are described (and describe their generation) – with important exceptions – as lacking in faith commitment, out of sympathy with the values and demands of the institutional Church. They experience the liturgy as boring, complicated and irrelevant to their concerns. The young emphasise their independence, sense of individual responsibility and demand for choice in matters of religion and morality. They set clear limits to authority. They are willing to acknowledge the personal authority of a priest within the context of a church service. Outside the narrow limits of the liturgy, the priest has no authority unless he is seen as a friend, someone they can look up to. Commenting on the priests in his parish one young person said, *"The young parish priests are in touch. Our 'old school' priests are on another planet."*

Young people are free of the pain, guilt and fear expressed by some older respondents in connection with disagreements about moral and sacramental issues. One young person commented that she thought her parents were almost too afraid to stand up and question the Church whereas she was quite opinionated. Another blamed parents for failing in their responsibilities. *"I don't think that it is that the Church doesn't appeal. It is parents and people's own point of view. Children shouldn't be allowed to do what they like. Parents promise to bring children up. They can't do it just so long as it is easy. Adults are not doing their job properly."*

Many adults praised young people for their latent spirituality and expressed optimism that, in time, they would return to the Church. Nevertheless, the common view, described by one young man, still at school, was that the Catholic identity of many of his generation was *"symbolic"*. It did not denote any faith commitment at all. Religion was not *"cool"*. Speaking personally, however, he indicated that his own attitudes had been formed and changed as a result of his schooling. He now had an understanding of the historical background to the Catholic tradition and a grasp of the reality of the person of Jesus. He was not alone among the young people interviewed in reporting a greater willingness to be involved in the Church as a result of sound education and formation. Some suggested that the Church lacks a forum in which the young can raise their genuine concerns. One young woman described her position a follows:

"My own age group does not see... the Church as having direct authority over them... A lot of people I talk to don't go to mass... there is massive unbelief... [We are] not taught what Rome says, we learn through our parents. There are a lot of things I don't agree with. Times are changing but Rome isn't. Doesn't realise it needs to move... I disagreed over one big issue. There was to be a family planning clinic in... There was uproar in this church, 'You cannot teach young people about contraception, it implies sex before marriage – which the Church is against.' But, times are changing, you can't stop it. It is better to have the contraception than an unwanted child and possibly abortion – which I am totally against. I agree with sex before marriage. Contraception and premarital sex go hand in hand. Sex is part of being with somebody, part of learning you are compatible. It is an important part of a relationship. It is up to the person."

In his theological reflection on **Diocesan Dispositions and Parish Voices** Fr. Kevin Kelly suggests that *"perhaps what is needed is not a mission to young people to convert them, but, rather putting more effort into listening to young people and into trying to learn from them about the meaning of the Gospel as they see it for today's world."*[41]

WOMEN DELIVER

Gender differences were also remarked upon. Women are regarded as exhibiting a greater faith commitment. They are said to exhibit a more nuanced approach to issues of authority, a greater willingness to compromise and to be involved in the life and work of the parish than are men. "Women deliver" said the authors of one parish report. At the same time, it is acknowledged that it is upon women that the personal costs of present authority structures and Church teaching bear most heavily. *"I still feel excluded from it all – particularly because of the lack of women in important positions."* Significantly, when women leave the Church, they take their children with them. Women and girls are seen as more reflective about issues of faith than males generally. The low level of male involvement is noted with concern. The employment situation is cited as one possible contributory factor. Men are said to be less sure of their place in society than hitherto. They are also said to be *"wary of the increasing involvement of women"* and see the Church as a *"female interest"* which contradicts their perception of masculinity.

COMMUNITY

CRYING FOR EACH OTHER'S SORROWS AND SHARING THEIR JOYS

The building up of the Catholic community in the various localities is among the most important of the priorities articulated by the priests interviewed. One said *"we prioritise faith formation and the development of the community. We have a lot on offer, a vision of a community of disciples."* The task presents considerable practical difficulties, but many parishioners speak well of their parishes in this respect. *"Very friendly, open and warm"* said one, *"you could never be lonely here"* said another. There is, however, an obvious temptation to identify the 'community' with regular mass-going Catholics and those most closely involved in parish life. *"The pity is that community spirit is centred around Mass"* said one deacon. The result can be an *"inward looking"* mentality and a sense of exclusion among those who, for whatever reason, are less engaged in parish life. *"People from outside feel it is a shut off."*

Lack of provision for and the engagement of young people in parish activities is a general concern – illustrated by the difficulty many parishes had in recruiting young people to take part in the survey. The attitude of the parish clergy and ability to relate to young people is highly significant. Some are gifted, others find it difficult to deal with teenagers. Several priests in the parishes studied had particular responsibilities for youth chaplaincy. One young man said that when the curate visited *"my parents talk about religion, but, I talk about anything. I respect him as a person. I talk to him like an older relation."* In one urban parish, affected by unemployment and ethnic tension, there is, according to the parish report "a general feeling that the priests genuinely like young people and make them feel valued". Unfortunately, the diocese does not always see youth ministry as a top priority. In another urban parish, the bishop had withdrawn the highly appreciated school chaplain, without notice, to provide cover for a situation elsewhere. Parishioners felt "powerless". The situation was made more difficult because, a young couple who had formerly been employed by the parish and "had made a great impact" upon the young had not been replaced.

As far as community building is concerned, relationships in rural parishes vary from the intimate *"we cry for each others sorrows and share their joys"* to the fragmented with people described as acquaintances rather than friends. Rural parishes experience difficulties because of their isolation, scattered populations, divided loyalties across villages, problems of communication and reluctance to travel far at night.

As noted above, reorganised parishes face the task of integrating different social groups with different outlooks and different views about the Church. Some joint parishes exhibit *"a bit of us and them... the two parishes are very different and holiday-makers affects it"*. One parish priest said that the people in one of his shared parishes are *"a deeply spiritual community"* upbeat and positive, whereas those in the linked parish are *"living in the past... prisoners of one another, in pigeon holes and scared to do something different."* Integration in such circumstances is a formidable challenge. Another priest commented that his two parishes are at very different stages of faith development. One parish has *"developed a mature sense of faith"* and is willing to accept responsibility. The other has *"a less developed sense of scripture"*. Yet another congregation is gradually emerging from a painful period of adjustment. A tightly knit, former industrial, village community, it has experienced the influx of predominantly middle class professionals from a new housing development. A lifelong resident commented *"there is a sense of community. There was resentment when people moved in... Shouldn't have been. I think things are getting better. People work hard for one another. It is good to see it. Fr..... has done well. He saw the problem and found the cure."* The cure has much to do with the commitment and warm outgoing personality of the parish priest as well as the fundamental goodwill of the local people.

The task of community development is a delicate one when previous priests have had personal problems. It is especially so when the trauma of suspected abuse has touched individual families; *"it came into my home"* said a parent. Rebuilding trust, confidence and stability takes time. The parish priest in another parish commented *"it's a tricky time for the parish... there will be a lot who feel isolated... we are feeling our way"*.

FEELING PART OF WHAT IS GOING ON

The more settled parishes are described as cohesive, welcoming and caring especially among 'same mass' communities. Enquiries by the interviewers reveal quite a complex picture. In one inner city parish, the openness, warmth and genuine spirituality of the parish priest is such that it influences the liturgy. *"You enjoy coming to mass here."* A service may be stopped to greet a newcomer. An elderly lady parishioner – by common consent the parish "leader" – is free, occasionally, to interrupt the service if, in the words of the interviewer, "she feels that a particular intention has been forgotten or if she has some other concern that needs to be raised". The difficulty is that the parish is highly dependent upon the outstanding personal qualities of its priest – who is also a hospital chaplain. His manifest gifts do not extend to planning for the future –

which includes the integration of another parish in a newly designated cluster. *"We just keep jogging along trying to hold on to what we've got."*

In contrast, another urban parish has made systematic and successful efforts over many years to generate *"a genuine spirit of community"*, a *"marrying of life experience and spirituality."* A large number of groups and activities has been developed reflecting the varied social composition of its different neighbourhoods. However, the initiative is beginning to run out of steam. There is confusion about whether the purpose of the neighbourhood groups is theological or social. There has been a shift from prayer and retreats to planning – *"It's more a cookbook approach with the same recipe provided."* Consequently, the spiritual impetus has withered – prompting the comment that now *"the parish are trailblazers to nowhere"*. The difficulties are compounded for the parish because the dedicated group of parishioners involved in leading the initiative, inspired by a forward looking parish priest twenty years ago, are now ageing. They are experiencing problems in identifying younger people willing to take over the responsibility for the future.

One settled parish is described as rather 'detached' in its approach to community, with *"individuals and groups… connected to the centre but not to each other"*. Parishioners confess that *"We are a massing community but not very developed in terms of Christian responsibility or relationships"*, *"we are a community in a middle class way"*. Importantly, echoing feedback from other parishes, the lack of any provision for young people means that *"they do not feel a part of what is going on"*. The distinction between the 'massing community' and others in the parish is evident in a different way in another parish where *"there is recognition and concern. You know people, they are friendly and warm."* Those within the small group contributing most to parish life *"feel a bond with people who attend mass with me"*. Here, these genuine bonds have rather set them apart from people whose connection with the Church is more tenuous. This inner core is seen by the interviewers as "potentially divisive", because, there is no "corporate sense of parish". Most of the congregation exhibit "complacency and passivity". As one parishioner remarked, *"Some feel excluded and some exclude themselves."* The parish is also seen as potentially vulnerable, because, as in other cases, "everything revolves around the parish priest… an open and collaborative pastor".

EXCEPTIONAL PRIESTS

As has been noted, most of the priests in charge of these parishes are exceptional. They need to be! As one parishioner said *"the priest can fill or empty a church today, people just vote with their feet".* Many parishioners voice anxiety about what will happen if their parish priest is moved. Some are still smarting from previous changes. In more than one case the anxiety is heightened by reservations about the attitudes of young priests who might take over. For example, the young curate in a successful parish is acknowledged to be enthusiastic and gifted but is seen as too conservative – in dress, liturgical preferences and preaching. *"According to him, the Church only recognises single people, celibates and people who have been married only once."*

The difficulties which can follow upon the replacement of a respected priest with someone who does not share his theology and approach to ministry are illustrated by Clare Barbour's account of a West London parish (not included in the Queen's study) *"Sadly, our parish priest died, and his successor had a very different concept of ministry, one which was equally instructive, though perhaps not quite for the same reasons. Within the space of a few weeks, or so it seemed, our parish community had shifted from being collaborative to hierarchical. This was achieved by our new pastor in two ways: first by the simple expedient of sidelining the parish-in-council to such an extent that its continuation would have caused an unChrist-like rift between priests and people had it not gracefully relinquished its perceived responsibilities. And secondly, by drawing all ministries into his own person: catechetics, talks and musical events, liturgy planning, bidding prayers and parish newsletter, ordering the church and deciding the times of Mass, all fell within his personal remit... I must confess to some astonishment at the speed with which our once active community, even while painfully conscious of their loss, withdrew once more into silent, passive obedience... But, as time passed I realised that perhaps my community was wiser than I. They had realised that sustained collaborative ministry at parish level is illusory; for without substantial structural change at the heart of the Church, its pastoral implementation is entirely within the 'gift' of the individual parish priests and for this reason will always remain cosmetic rather than systemic"*[42]

Fortunately, relationships with the priests, in the parishes surveyed, are generally very good, even excellent. They rate high praise from their people. They are variously described as happy, open, approachable, appreciative, flexible, caring, deeply spiritual, good at listening and communicating. *"...he empowers people"*, *"He's number one, a magnet, super guy, and good at encouraging people"*, *"He exudes holiness and goodness; he has a great ability to draw people"*, *"I've never met two better examples of the Gospel"*. They are regarded as competent, committed, frequently strong characters, unwilling to tolerate factions and sometimes, unsettling. *"We have a born leader who believes in delegating and consulting"*, *"a team leader and a man of vision"*. There is little direct criticism.

What little there is tends to come from those unhappy with the style of leadership, *"It's good but we don't see eye to eye"* or from those who are in the unhappier half of a joint parish. One priest in a joint parish with two churches, which had been through much difficulty, commented about the disaffected congregation *"the parish priest is not viewed as human… I found it hard to get into their skins"*. Part of the problem, he believes is his class and background. In the other church community he is held in such high regard that the interviewer commented "Attitudes… were so different as almost to make Fr..... seem like two people."

One of the difficulties which arise when exceptional priests are in charge of parishes, is that the community can begin to mirror their strengths and weaknesses. An example is the case where the priest is *"not an organiser, but gets so much done by force of personality"* – *"we need to be pinned down in discussion, with others, to unpack and plan a strategy"*. Another example is when a dominant priest has what one parish report described as, "inherent difficulties combining the roles of pastor, organiser and manager". Again, when the priest acts *"as the social cement for the community"*, parishioners come to rely on his contribution. Dependence is actually increased and the parish becomes vulnerable to a change of personnel. Such examples illustrate the need for shared responsibility and – as Clare Barbour has noted – the structural changes necessary to achieve genuine collaborative ministry. As one parishioner put it *"parishioners stay, priests don't."*

LEADERSHIP, PARTICIPATION AND FORMATION IN THE PARISH

BURN OUT

Leadership, participation and formation are dealt with in detail in Annette Barker's booklet in the series.[43] As expected, particularly given the calibre of the men, parishioners unanimously identify their parish priest as the key person in the parish. It is also clear that, however conscientious they are about consultation and *"attempt seriously to involve people in the decision making process"*, the priests reserve to themselves the responsibility for the final decision. Reasons vary. Many parishioners still expect the priest to do so even in cases where it is not necessary – or even prudent. They see the parish priest as ultimately accountable in a way that they are not. For most priests it is what the job demands and is also a requirement of canon law. For some, it is simply the most efficient way to work. For others, it may be a very significant aspect of their priesthood or a consequence of the force of their personality. *"The parish priest gives the impression of letting parishioners get on with it, but, in fact, he is very controlling"*, *"...if someone isn't happy, he'll challenge them and then wear them down"*. Given the workloads that their priests carry, parishioners may voice concern that they *"will burn themselves out before too long"*, *"we are killing our priests, we have less of them and yet we expect the same"*. Such concerns are not, however, manifested in a marked willingness to share the burdens – by both parties.

A PASSIVE PEOPLE OR COMMITTED BUT DISENGAGED?

Parishioners may wish to be consulted and kept well informed. But – as was noted in *Part One* – most are reluctant to accept responsibility and become deeply involved in parish activities. As one report noted "there does not seem a great desire among parishioners for greater participation in the life of the Church. The most common responses were... *"most people are passive they want things done for them"*... *"they are afraid of involvement"*. In the majority of parishes studied, a small group of, perhaps, between a dozen and fifty parishioners, participate fully. Significantly, this means that 80%-95% of **active** churchgoers are not involved. The labourers are indeed few. These results cannot be generalised to the Catholic population as a whole. But, if they were repeated elsewhere, it would mean that no more than 1%-8% of the estimated total Catholic population is fully engaged in parish life. A potentially very worrying statistic.

In a small minority of parishes the proportion of actively involved mass attenders is higher at around one third, but this was rare. One parish, nevertheless, reported 100 eucharistic ministers. Reference has already been made to another parish which embarked upon a programme of parish renewal twenty years ago under an inspirational parish priest. It has achieved significant success. But, the initiative is beginning to falter. In the words of the parish report, "Concern was repeatedly expressed at the difficulties of sustaining commitment in the face of declining numbers, ageing membership, occupational and family pressures, and – to a degree – diminishing enthusiasm, as those individuals who had been inspired by the original... initiative aged and were not replaced". The parish is fortunate to have another very able, pastorally committed, parish priest as successor to the man who was responsible for the original programme. He is aware of the issues and has the confidence to tackle them.

Sound reasons can be advanced for the lack of involvement of most Catholics in their parishes.

- First, there is the historical legacy of a dependent Catholic laity – *"they are so used to being excluded they won't go forward"*.

- Second, as has been noted, social change has led to more critical and discerning attitudes to the Church. Some people are inhibited about active involvement because of disagreements over teaching or sincerely held concerns about justice within the structures of the Church. Others are inhibited because they are not in good standing with the authorities and/or because of a feeling of unworthiness in view of their circumstances and attitudes. People can feel 'defined out' of active involvement.

- Third, there are the preoccupations of parishioners with the economic and social changes affecting their lives. There is *"not enough time in people's lives today to get involved in the Church, the pressure of work etc. is too great"*. In Britain, over ninety per cent of men and seventy per cent of women are in paid employment. Families are more scattered as a result of increased mobility and the demands of their jobs. Just keeping in touch takes people away from their parishes. In addition, parents are now faced with growing responsibilities for dependent relatives. Children are dependent longer due to educational change, student debt and the cost of setting up home. The elderly are dependent as a result of improved life expectancy but increasing frailty or chronic ill health as they age. As Sarah Lindsell reminds us, two-thirds of all care is given within the family and one in eight people in Britain is now a carer[44].

- Fourth, the focus of much parish life is inward looking and narrow – sometimes even trivial – when compared to the exacting demands of work, worrying family responsibilities and contemporary, intractable, social problems. *"The Church looks after its own members and expects other people to come to it."* When questioned about the issues which were under discussion in the parish, the changes which had taken place and the decisions which had recently been made, parishioners mentioned: the timing of masses; changing arrangements for celebrating first communion; reordering the sanctuary; plans for halls and car parks. Such issues can raise storms of protest and result in months of argument. Busy people could be forgiven for believing that such matters can safely be left to others (who may regard them as important and rewarding), provided they are given an opportunity to make their views known.

- Fifth, motivated and challenging people may have disengaged from active Church life, disappointed or exhausted. In one of the personal testimonies prepared for the Queen's Foundation project, a formerly active lay woman commented *"Given the way power is exercised in the Church, working for change involves either seeking to influence those who hold power or confronting them. My experience of the influencing process is that it consumes all creative energy and much time for very little perceptible result... I abandoned – or at least ceased to give priority to – the let's change (the institution of) the church option... We must listen to God's word... that word is most loudly whispered among the poor and oppressed. For me it follows therefore, that whatever skills and energy I have must be put at the disposal of the dispossessed."*[45]

● Finally, people know that, under the present system, the ultimate decision will almost certainly be taken by the parish priest, *"if the parish priest wants to do it, it will be done anyway."*

These difficulties are not insoluble, but they will take time. The solution entails appropriate formation (both lay and clerical), structural change and pastoral sensitivity. In Fr. Kevin Kelly's view, it will also require *"a growing awareness in the Church that, unless priests are open to some form of accountability, the Vatican II notion of corresponsibility, consultation and collaborative ministry will ring very hollow."* He favours a parish mission statement *"decided upon and owned by the parish as a whole and which any incoming priest has a responsibility to accept."*[46] Those with skill and enthusiasm who have disengaged will need to be re-integrated. People must believe that the parish is addressing really important issues. They need to identify with the priority given to specific problems and the possible solutions. They must also experience a willingness among the Church authorities both to be fully inclusive in drawing upon its members and to confirm them in the exercise of genuine power and responsibility. Fr. John Armitage notes the leadership difficulties and skill shortages experienced in inner-city parishes but says *"I feel sometimes that we are pressing the wrong buttons."* He quotes the example of his own East-London parish. *"A few years ago, after another attempt at forming a parish council had died a death, I was approached and asked if we could take part in a night shelter scheme with some local churches. My response was that if there were enough people who wanted to take part we would be happy to be involved. I asked for volunteers, and in my pessimism I said that we would meet in the presbytery, not expecting very many. Nearly forty people turned up and we are now in our fifth year... The night shelter has been a wonderful work in our parish."*[47] But, as will be seen, many parishes have a very limited view of civic involvement and its relevance to the mission of the parish.

Parishioners are not only reluctant to accept responsibility for running the parish, they are also hesitant to engage in adult religious formation, *"a lot of Catholics are frightened of getting in too deep"*. One of the reports described the majority of parishioners as "spiritually unawakened". *"The need is there but we haven't figured out the right way of doing it yet"*. Most Catholics appear comfortable with the level of faith formation received at school *"there is not much interest from parishioners in pursuing their inner life"*. There is little appetite for systematic adult faith development. *"I'm OK. You're asking too deep a question"* said one. *"Those who want it can find it"* said another. Also, it has to be said, provision is haphazard. But, one middle aged lady spoke of the effect of being woken up spiritually *"Once you got a taste for it you wanted more... you start addressing yourself... You think you are doing great until you get that wee bit of awakening... you cannot be satisfied with formal prayer after that... you need to go deeper, deeper."*

Those undertaking parish ministries readily acknowledge that they are valued and encouraged. Practical support and training is much less in evidence, with the exception perhaps of eucharistic ministers. Many had been 'thrown in at the deep end'. In fact, despite RCIA programmes, a few courses, occasional initiatives at diocesan and parish level – and the efforts of the small number of dedicated but hard pressed diocesan adult religious education staff, – the resources devoted to adult formation are very limited. Consequently, there is little systematic, accessible and affordable provision at parish or diocesan level. Much that is available appeals to a relatively educated minority. Speaking about their willingness to attend formation courses one person said *"it would have to be my kind of people. The retreats and so on are for intellectual people."* Another commented *"the thing I always disliked about courses was that the language was difficult for some people to understand. They could have made things simpler."*

The conclusion to the report on one of the most active and successful parishes could be applied to most of the others. "The parish needs to reflect carefully on its likely future situation... There is a clear mismatch between the present, somewhat haphazard, adult religious formation experiences and the kind of formation necessary to sustain the parish in the future. There is also a sense of disengagement amongst the younger members of the parish, and combined with the ageing group of active participants and falling congregations, there may be some difficulty in replacing these individuals when they step down." Fr. Kevin Kelly argues that a thorough review of expenditure on religious formation at diocesan level will be a key element in any solution, *"talk about more comprehensive lay-involvement will not be credible to people unless they see that their diocese is embracing such a development positively and enthusiastically. And that means adequate resource allocation. To many, including myself, that means making the budget for the training of priests merely one item, and not necessarily the most important item, within the budget for ministerial formation in general. It also means situating the formation of priests within the wider human context of formation... thereby reducing the danger of priests seeing themselves as 'men apart'..."*[48] Such a review would, however, need to be conducted in the light of the issues raised by Philip Grindell in his discussion of the ability of the local Church to meet its financial obligations and the implications for parish congregations.

MISSION

THE TEACHING OF VATICAN II

The conciliar Decree on the Church's Missionary Activity 'Ad Gentes' affirms that the Church is by its very nature missionary. It is charged with enabling all men and women to participate in the 'saving mystery of Christ'; offering them the opportunity of peace and communion with God and their fellow men. The Dogmatic Constitution on the Church 'Lumen Gentium' makes it clear that the Church is truly present in all legitimately organised local groups of the faithful, no matter how small or poor. Lumen Gentium also states that *"each disciple of Christ has the obligation of spreading the faith to the best of their abilities"*, nurturing human dignity, solidarity and freedom. The 1971 Synod of Bishops indicated that justice and the transformation of the world were central to the Gospel message and to mission. In 1975, Pope Paul VI in his Apostolic Exhortation "Evangelisation in the Modern World" affirms that this requires both radical interior personal transformation through conversion of heart and transformation of the social and political order to ensure liberation from everything that oppresses. The late Fr. George Soares-Prabhu reminds us that change of heart without a change of structure leaves oppression unchanged, while a change of structure alone will lead to new forms of oppression through greed and selfishness. *"The vision of Jesus summons us, then, to ceaseless struggle."*[49]

THE CHURCH OF LAODICEA

The parishes are full of people of goodwill. Many of those surveyed have serious problems of their own with which to contend. Yet, judged by the standards of the Council Fathers and the exhortation of Paul VI, the majority of parishes surveyed are at an immature stage of development. They are predominantly inward-looking and have narrow, 'churchy' preoccupations. Awareness of the extent of the Christian missionary obligation or vocation is limited. The celebration of Mass for the worshipping community is central to their concerns. Mission is primarily seen in terms of generosity towards appeals for funds, the work of the SVP, contact with lapsed Catholics, responding to enquirers through the RCIA programmes and limited ecumenical witness. Parishes have very little active engagement with civil society – apart from the statutory education authorities. Fr. Kevin Kelly asks whether the inward looking nature of parishes may be *"one reason why many young people feel that our Church does not speak to them and their concerns? Maybe they are not interested in belonging to a community whose main focus is the security and welfare of its members?"*[50]

The parishes in the survey rarely act corporately as 'the local Church' to tackle social problems – pro-life witness would be an occasional exception. Parishioners are left to pursue their interest in social and political objectives through mainly secular channels or Catholic Charities outside the parish. Thus, reference is made to *"RC's who are in professional or caring jobs… or of the more invisible caring carried out by parishioners in the neighbourhood"*. It would be wrong to underestimate the importance of individual expression of the ethic of universal social concern through charitable work. As has already been noted, Christians of all denominations comprise the majority of the workforce, paid and unpaid, in organised charitable activity. But, this is largely undertaken independently of their parishes and only a minority consciously identify their religious beliefs as a motive for their involvement.[51]

Most parishioners are positive about ecumenism, but, there are suggestions that the energy invested in initiatives has diminished in recent years. Relations with other churches are generally cordial, but not intimate and rarely entail sustained social contact. In some areas a legacy of anti-Catholic feeling remains which can affect attitudes. Catholic approaches to a neighbouring church had been rebuffed as unwelcome in one parish. In another, the fortress mentality among older residents was such that, *"We are not yet at a stage where we can be ecumenical."* Clergy attend periodic meetings with other Christian ministers. The quality of relationships varies with the commitment and personality of the parish priest. A small minority of lay people is involved in Lenten discussion groups, Easter processions of witness, or occasional inter-church services such as the Women's World Day of Prayer. In general, the priority given to Church unity is not high. *"Ecumenism? It's OK if they join us… I don't think I'm prepared to compromise"* was one response. Others are embarrassed by the lack of progress, *"We are dancing round the edges."*

Mission, in the sense of sustained outreach and involvement in the local community, is not developed at all. *"No one sits down and asks 'What are we here for'"*. One parishioner suggested that the lack of 'clear missionary intent' echoed *"the situation higher up the Church"*. Some Catholics regard mission in purely spiritual terms or equate it with priests attracting more people into Church. *"We are open, if you want to come in, come in."* Others simply state *"This is not a missionary parish"*, or say *"I do not think the parish accepts a responsibility to wider society. It has no organisations"*. Others confirm that *"Individuals do good things, but not as a group"* and that there is *"No motivation, no push."* *"People would not notice if the Catholics were blown away tomorrow!"* Their insularity may even be defended, in the words of one parish report, "as a positive thing." People may see the Church as *"a haven from life"* and *"for personal salvation"*. They may suggest that the parish exists *"to support the local Roman Catholic population and their families"* maintaining that it *"is not the place to outreach from... evangelisation should take place in the schools"*.

Fortunately, others see the situation differently, sometimes inspired by the example of their priests. They acknowledge, as one parish report noted "that there was, or should be, a particular mission to the local neighbourhood, but it had never been properly articulated". *"We really need to show that we love everyone of every colour, race or faith"*. In this parish, the assistant priest drew praise for his efforts to build bridges with the Asian community in an area beset with racial tension. But, significantly, the report reserved judgement about the effect on the parish by stating "To what extent the parish as a whole share his obvious concern or are behind his efforts, however, remains an open question". Another parish priest is motivated by a strong personal sense of mission and desire to be a *"gospel presence"* in his multi-racial locality. He is indebted to a religious priest who helps him out and has built up a foundation of goodwill in the area. The parish report confirms that "his personal conviction has established itself in the general mentality of the congregation". As yet, the contribution remains ad hoc. *"There is a vision about parish involvement, but, no planning."*

In considering the response of active Catholics to the challenge of mission, one is reminded of a comment by Michael Fogarty. He noted that, in comparison to those who remained active, Christians who had disengaged from the institutional Churches tended to be enthusiastic and critical, with drive and a capacity to get results. Weekly church attenders on the other hand conveyed *"just a hint of the Church of Laodicea"*.[52] And we know what the Lord said to them! *" I know your deeds, that you are neither cold nor hot. I wish you were either one or the other! So, because you are lukewarm – neither hot nor cold – I am about to spit you out of my mouth."*[53]

These tendencies, and concern about them, are not confined to Britain. Mgr. Philip Murnion commenting upon a conference on parish life in the Americas, notes *"the representatives of parishes in fifteen countries shared concern that parishes could settle into themselves and become contented communities of mutual care. They hoped that parishes would both reach out to the most marginal persons in their communities and acquire a critical perspective on their own culture and personal lives… the culture the Church lives in needs the kind of careful analysis one brings to missionary work. For parishioners and parish leaders have become strangers to their own culture, too often oblivious to the ways that culture is shaping us and too often co-opted by that culture. Furthermore, parishes too often have withdrawn into themselves, attentive to their own needs and unaware of the needs of others who are not in the pews for Sunday Mass."*[54] He is anxious nevertheless, not to overstate the problem and underestimate the good that is being done locally. He also notes that adopting the notion of a missionary community as a vision for the future involves a tension. The source of the tension is the need to deepen community ties whilst at the same time using the community as the *"agent and context of the outreach to and initiation of new members"*.

RELATIONSHIPS WITH THE LOCAL DIOCESE

BISHOPS AND THE TWO-SPEED DIOCESES

There is a remarkable uniformity of opinion about relationships between parish and diocese. This is despite the variety of regional, economic and social conditions within the twelve parishes surveyed. As with the pope and the Roman curia, parishioners distinguish between the person of the bishop, and the administration of the diocese. The bishop is usually (but not universally) liked and respected, often seen as able, approachable or down to earth, but not necessarily businesslike. *"If he ran a business like he runs the diocese he would be sacked."* He is, sometimes, regarded as too passive and indecisive, too likely *"to flit from flower to flower"* or, in one case, too unreflective and outspoken. Some parishioners appear to be aware of their bishop's personal interests and pastoral concerns; e.g. third world poverty; the homeless; the handicapped, single parents and so on.

The diocese, on the other hand, is mostly seen as impersonal, faceless, and like Rome *"out of touch"*. Part of the explanation may lie in the tensions which develop in large organisations between head office and branches or in the common frustration of ordinary people with bureaucracy. But, the gulf between diocese and parish is serious and worrying, particularly given the significance of the diocese within the theology of the local Church. One report described the relationship as "unclear, fearful and disconnected", another as "strained". *"You don't feel that this parish is too important as far as the diocese goes. There is plenty of loyalty to the bishop."* Parishioners generally do not have a high regard for the diocesan authorities. *"I have a poor opinion of the way the diocese is run. It is far too priest and religious oriented. Young people are the future and should be a priority but they are not." "The diocese has two speeds; dead slow and stop!"* Decisions taken by diocesan authorities are sometimes perceived as impositions at parish level. This causes resentment. Some contrast the more open decision-making processes in their parish with their experience of high-handed diocesan procedures. One parish priest commented that there is *"no sense that the diocese listens, wants to listen or knows how to listen… there have been many missed opportunities"*. Dissatisfaction was expressed about one bishop who *"makes empty promises"*, *"he doesn't care and doesn't like people standing up to him"*.

NOTHING BONDS

Contact with the diocese is limited and it does not feature large in the consciousness of most parishioners – apart from its financial demands. *"We haven't a sense of diocese"*, *"If the diocese did not exist we would not notice"*. *"There is not much diocesan impact… except the diocesan debt and the levy"*. *"They readily accept our surplus funding"*. An exception is the very small minority with some diocesan responsibility – for example school governors or those who attend courses and events. As one person put it, *"unless you are particularly involved in the diocese, there isn't a relationship at all"*. At best, connections are described as *"amicable but not close"*, at worst apathetic. People are vague about the nature of the relationship between the diocese and the parish, *"the diocese has too much to do and is out of touch."* In most cases, people struggle to think of any links. *"No bad feelings but no-one from the diocese is ever seen around here doing things."* One comment summed up many of the opinions expressed, *"nothing bonds with the diocese"*. The theology of the Local Church clearly sits uneasily with the reality.

IS THERE A PLAN?

Some parishes believe that lack of contact is partly due to the fact that they are geographically remote from the centre of diocesan operations and partly due to whether they are troublesome – or not. Thus, one parish suggested that they heard little from the diocese because they were *"very remote… quiet, well behaved, not in debt, not stroppy."* Conversely, another parish thought it was because they had been seen as a *"nuisance"*. Other communities regarded themselves as *"forgotten"*, *"we get a raw deal"*. Importantly, the diocese is not seen as relevant to the faith life of the community. *"I am a member of a local Catholic community; not an institutionalised Church."*

Familiarity and responsibility can change these negative perceptions. One respondent who had been appointed a diocesan trustee said, *"I am starting to get a wider picture… I'm seeing an awful lot of change in the Church"*. The majority, however, including those in the diocese just mentioned, confess to being uninformed about the plans and priorities of their bishop. Many (including the priests themselves) doubt that there is any planning. *"I'm not aware of any priorities if there are any" "There is no clear strategy".* *"Is there a plan? If so there is great lack of communication."* Even those involved with the diocesan authorities feel confused by lack of feedback. They conclude that no systematic planning is taking place. This was the case even in a parish which had recently undergone reorganisation at the behest of the diocese – despite the parish priest encouraging his congregation to inform themselves better. Almost nobody claims intimate knowledge. Those who believe that they are reasonably well informed are not impressed. *"I am aware of the vision and shortage of priests, but, nothing is being done."* Many are not really interested. *"The diocese is pushed too much. Church is parish to ordinary people; anything else is structure."* The diocesan authorities thus appear to have limited impact other than through the mediation of priests. A number of those interviewed suggested that lack of contact suited all involved. Except, of course, when priests are moved without consultation or parishes closed!

CONSULTATION

Lack of consultation is a cause of resentment – especially over appointments, parish reorganisation and closure. Several of the parishes in the study had experienced merger or clustering. Others had coped with a succession of priests with difficult problems – emotional, sexual and alcohol abuse. One parish had experienced five changes of parish priest in ten years. One reason, it was suggested, was because the parish did not treat its priests very well. The impact was profound, but, appeals to the dean and the bishop apparently fell on deaf ears. Parishioners were not kept informed. They felt let down, particularly because they believed that, had the diocese taken them seriously, one of the priests would not have suffered a breakdown. As it was, the priest suddenly departed. The parish was left to cope for 15 weeks largely on its own. Significantly, the Easter liturgy organised by the parishioners was described in the parish report as "meaningful and enriching". The new parish priest is viewed positively, especially in relation to his contact with young people, but also holds a time consuming diocesan appointment. He invites opinions on long term parish development but, according to the report "does not seem committed". He is seen as inexperienced and *"learning the ropes"*. This has led him, parishioners believe, to make errors of judgement.

'BULLSHIT FROM HQ!'

Communication is generally acknowledged to be poor and in need of improvement. Letters from the diocese may be read at mass and extracts may appear in the weekly parish bulletin. Information is more likely to be gleaned from the media than directly from the diocese. Parishioners would prefer to hear the details from their bishop – especially if there is bad news. Two serious examples of the effect of the failure of communication and relationships in 'bad news' situations were obtained. It is important to recall, nevertheless, that, in both cases, the bishop himself had courageously nominated the parish for study. It is also important to emphasise that parishioners exercised much charity, concern and sensitivity in describing the events to the interviewers.

The first parish had experienced a succession of three priests all with problems. One had been arrested. Those responsible for interviews in the parish remarked upon the care parishioners took to avoid gossip and to consider what was an appropriate response to their enquiries. One parishioner took several days to reflect before agreeing to discuss details of one of the cases. None sought to stigmatise the priests. Indeed, emphasis was given to what the events revealed about the ordinary humanity of the priests and their needs. The report on the parish summarises the position as follows:

"...the parish had undergone 'catastrophic changes. The most serious of these was the arrest of the parish priest. The situation was described as sordid. It devastated the parish, caused factions and confusion... loyalties were stretched... Another priest disappeared for long periods without explanation. Coupled with this were the sudden theological changes which accompanied the parish priests and their substitutes during unsettled times... the parish lost direction... 'it felt like a broken marriage'.[55]

"The majority felt let down by the diocese, 'Bullshit from HQ and all hearsay in the parish'. Nothing was announced. The diocese might as well not have existed. There was no leadership from the diocese and parishioners felt ignorant of the facts. There was no opportunity for lay leadership during these crises. There was poor communication between parish and diocese. Many believed that the diocese let the situation go on for too long, that the true nature of the previous priest's difficulties must have been known and that inaction caused unnecessary suffering, to the priests themselves as well as to the people. Some parishioners regretted that no structure was in place to deal with the situation, despite the fact that some claimed people did get in touch with the diocese.

"There was great anger in the parish and without leadership one parishioner claimed that people turned in on themselves in a destructive way... part of the community just slipped away during the periods of uncertainty.

"The people believe that the diocese did not know what to do... the indecision from the diocese was obvious and consequently the people had a poor opinion of the way the diocese handled changes... the parish felt outside the diocese, 'excluded as if we'd been put on hold and didn't exist'. Some claimed they never saw the bishop during this time."

The second parish was attempting to cope with a merger. The former, much loved parish priest admitted to an abuse scandal. The parish was traumatised, undermining trust and opportunities to unify it with the neighbouring church congregation. It placed the new parish priest in an extremely difficult and delicate position. The parish was not prepared for a new appointment. One parishioner described the situation as *"like a death"*, some parishioners *"won't come back to the Church."* Another person said *"there is no anger against Fr....., just extreme sadness"*, others commented:

"We've not been told the whole truth and people feel hurt. The bishop was aware of the situation. The [new] parish priest kept a small group informed and gave out information when necessary. For the future they must involve the whole community."

"The bishop should have paid more attention to Fr.....'s outward state as it indicated an inward problem... It's a nightmare for the new Parish Priest. There are no guidelines. He had the press at the door, no help from the bishop. He had to face people and they felt abandoned. There was total bitterness. Fr..... could have been honest with the people, but wasn't. Now we have to settle down and get on with the job – we have to."

The experience, though avoidable with sensitive handling, has soured relationships with the diocese. People feel that their bishop offered no initial support and left them without explanations. The diocesan response is seen as too little too late. *"We're isolated"*, *"We're not happy with the bishop"*, *"We need to see the bishop more often"*, *"there's confrontation, stonewalling and central control"*. Parishioners also express anxiety about the burden placed upon the new parish priest *"the diocese asks too much… probably just as Rome asks too much of the bishop."* Nevertheless, by nominating the parishes concerned for inclusion in the study, it is clear that the bishops involved in both cases are aware of the problems created and anxious that important lessons should be learned.

THE CRY OF COLLECTIVE PAIN

In his theological reflection on the parish studies, Fr. Kevin Kelly refers to the Dutch theologian Fr. Edward Schillebeeckx who *"coined the expression 'contrast experience'. By that he meant a kind of collective cry of pain which erupts from people when they are faced by what is not in keeping with their deepest humanity. It is as though some very profound instinct is crying out: 'This should not be. This is not how life should be lived'. I get the impression that in many of the parishes interviewed, the lack of any coherent pastoral policy on the part of the diocese is experienced as a kind of contrast experience… If this is the case, such a cry of pain would be extremely important theologically. It could perhaps be interpreted as God's creative Spirit crying out from the grass-roots of the Church and calling for renewal at local and diocesan level."* [56]

PART THREE: WHAT NOW?

OBVIOUS QUESTIONS

AUTHENTICITY AND USEFULNESS

The foregoing account of change, communication and relationships in the Catholic Church has attempted to convey something of the reality of contemporary parish life and to set it within a wider social and religious context. The assessment is not, however, based upon a scientifically representative sample of churchgoers. Rather, it is the product of a series of conversations with about 100 senior diocesan personnel in six dioceses and some 350 priests and parishioners from twelve parishes within those dioceses. An immediate question arises. *"Is the picture conveyed an authentic one?"* The research team believe it is. Christians from other denominations have also suggested that similar results could have been obtained from within their own congregations[57]. The real test, however, is whether the account 'resonates' with bishops, priests and people in other parishes and other dioceses. Whether, perhaps, they recognise something of themselves and their own situation in the record of the conversations, or whether they regard the experiences of the dioceses and parishes studied as too unrepresentative to be accurate and helpful. It is hoped that the material presented in the booklet will, at least, provide a basis for serious reflection at parish level.

Two related and obvious questions concern the usefulness of the exercise. *"Don't we know it already and what use is it anyway?"* Informed observers will, of course, be well aware of specific findings from the enquiry. What is new is the scope and comprehensiveness of the study. Part of the usefulness of a systematic account of the present situation is that appreciation of the complexities involved will help guard against 'quick fixes'. Also, hints at appropriate solutions to some of the problems may be contained in what, it is hoped, is an objective, but not unsympathetic, consideration of the issues. The implications for our previous assumptions and for the viewpoints we cherish may, however, be uncomfortable.

FORMIDABLE CHALLENGES

MISMATCH

It may be helpful, therefore, briefly to rehearse some of the main themes of the report. First, as A H Halsey suggests, social change transformed people's lives in the twentieth century and changed attitudes to authority. We may mourn for aspects of the past, but, the world will not be the same again. As far as the Catholic Church is concerned, there is a mismatch between contemporary values (*autonomy, equality, openness, participation, tolerance, protest*) and the dominant institutional view of the lay person as ultimately *dependent* upon the power and authority of an exclusively male priesthood. The most active Catholics are women and the contrast is especially sharp and painful for them.

DISAPPEARING BABIES

Second, the demographic structure of the Church has changed and will continue to do so on present trends, influenced, in part, by national fertility and marriage rates. Active priests and mass attending parishioners are an ageing and diminishing group. The number of Catholic marriages fell from around 12 per year for every 1000 Catholics in Britain in the 1940's, to around 3 per year in the late 1990's. This has serious implications for long term Catholic family formation as well as for religious vocations. In the same period, infant baptisms declined from about 30 per 1000 Catholics each year to 15 per thousand. The implications need to be faced by the Church community as a whole. That will be difficult.

SQUEEZING THE BISHOP

Third, the emphasis of the Second Vatican Council upon the Church as a community gathered around its bishop, has not been realised in practice. On the one hand, the size and complexity of dioceses prevent it. On the other, the authority of the bishops has diminished. It has been squeezed between a centralising papacy and an unreformed Roman Curia within the *institution* and changing social attitudes within the *parishes*. There are theological, structural and pastoral issues to be addressed.

GROWN-UP CATHOLICS

Fourth, as lay Catholics, we must be prepared to 'grow-up' theologically and spiritually with all that is entailed. It will mean accepting the implications of our baptismal vocation and ceasing to expect a pastoral 'free ride' at the expense both of our priests and the committed minority of ageing active parishioners. It will almost certainly involve an uncomfortable period of adjustment for all concerned, including episodes of disagreement and confrontation – hopefully in charity. Among the clergy, the discomfort will perhaps be felt most acutely by those who were formed in and for a very different Church and those who fall into Noel Timms category of *sacred priests in a closed Church*. It will certainly be difficult for most lay people, if the passivity and lack of a sense of mission emerging from the enquiry is common in places other than the twelve parishes surveyed. On the other hand, those who have experienced a spiritual awakening have been transformed by it. They have made an impact upon their parishes, especially when working with an inspiring and visionary pastor. The possibility to exercise a genuine vocation, to tackle – with the active support of the local Church – issues that are at the heart of community and religious life could help revitalise the Church. It might dispel the mentality of the Church of Laodicea that caught the attention of Michael Fogarty. It could shift us away from the narrow, rather shrivelled, pre-occupations of current parish life towards a fuller, richer understanding of *mission*. It might also attract back to active participation some of the more dynamic, challenging and prophetic characters who have sought to fulfill their vocation in the secular sphere, or retreated to the margins of the Church. Such developments will require *a conversion of heart* and will need to be facilitated by structural change.

PASTORAL SENSITIVITY AND STRUCTURAL CHANGE

When we want to know what a person really values, we attend closely to the way they behave. As Fr. J Mahoney has pointed out, " *The Church's primary mission so far as it concerns morality is not to propound it but to exemplify it… by working to be itself what it is called to be. The Church is its message; its being is its witness… The Church is called to be a 'mirror to grace'… so that those human qualities which appear lacking or dim in society at large may be shown in the Church.*" Such qualities will be manifest he suggests in its constitution, the experience of fellowship (both within the Church and when reaching out to others) and in the building up of the community.[58] What values does the institutional Church communicate to the world – in the way it treats its members, fellow Christians of other denominations, those of other faith traditions and those of no faith at all? Focusing primarily upon internal relationships, people in the parishes raise questions about the degree to which the institution exemplifies in its *practice* the Gospel values it proclaims in its *teaching*. As has been seen, they express concern about, for example, the exercise of some aspects of authority, the treatment of women, the experience of the divorced and others deemed to be in error. They are dismayed by poor communication; scandalised by inaction and apparent secrecy in cases of abuse. They seek sensitivity to the local context, desire transparency in administration and accountability among those who exercise

51

responsibility in the Church. Significantly, in a number of respects, the human qualities of which Fr. Mahoney speaks are dim *within* the Church rather than *manifested* by it when compared to secular society. Despite widespread anxiety about the values of our urban, industrialised, capitalist societies, it has actually been the secular state and commercial organisations that have led the way in Britain: in encouraging opportunities for human development, participation and the exercise of responsibility; in legislating to prevent child abuse, racial or sexual discrimination; in promoting high standards in education and social services; in improving the quality of financial stewardship within institutions; in promoting employee welfare and in developing best practice terms and conditions of employment;. There is, clearly, work to be done if the Church is to be truly a 'mirror to grace' for wider society.

MAKING CONNECTIONS

The implications for the Local Church can be summarised as a set of formidable challenges. All are manageable given goodwill, a strong and holy spirit. They do, however, involve the *vital pastoral space* Cardinal Kaspar has demanded for bishops, and a greater willingness to trust in the fundamental goodness of ordinary Catholics.

- At Diocesan level, these include: *developing a coherent Local Church identity and sense of common purpose; adult spiritual and religious formation; the continuing (joint) formation of clergy and laity; clarifying pastoral priorities; formulating and integrating pastoral strategy and financial planning; reconciling the demands of canon law and civil law; reforming structures to be consistent with baptismal vocation and mission; improving communications; investing in human-resource-management skills and raising clergy morale.*
- At Parish level, they include: *re-connecting with the diocese and with the universal Church in a way that does justice to common sense, personal experience and the needs of the wider Church; careful reflection on 'Mission' and the implications of a baptismal vocation; expanding the narrow horizons of parish life; accepting full adult responsibility for the life and vitality of the parish community, its links with local churches and with civil society.*

A touch more democracy in Church government would help! E Schillebeeckx has questioned why the Church *"should not be able to democratise its model of government and rule without in doing so harming its subjection to the Word of God?"* It had, after all, adapted to feudal and monarchical forms.[59]

APPENDIX

THE AUTHORITY AND GOVERNANCE PROJECT

The project began in 1996 at the Queen's Foundation For Ecumenical Theological Education, Birmingham. It is concerned with the nature, exercise and experience of authority and the practise of government in the Roman Catholic Church. The aims are to assist the Church address the complex problems of authority, governance, relationships and participation in contemporary Britain and, where appropriate, to adapt pastoral policy and practice. The baptismal vocation of lay people is a particular concern. How, for example, do we distinguish the authority that is a *baptismal right and responsibility* of all Christians from that which follows from *orders and office* in the Church? The process has been informed by careful theological reflection and enriched by the everyday experience of ordinary Catholics.

A conversational methodology has been adopted – open, generous and respectful – drawing upon the views and experience of bishops, priests, theologians and ordinary lay Catholics. About 1000 people have been consulted. Special attention has been given to those groups whose circumstances lead them to experience the authority of the Church more acutely than others e.g. the divorced, those married to Christians of other denominations, ethnic minorities, priests and religious no longer active in ministry and women. The project involves surveys of the opinions of bishops, priests and people. Importantly, it also entails theological reflection, publication of results and dissemination of the findings at local level within the Church. A list of the various publications is included as an appendix.

The research has been directed by a specialist working party. The members are able to offer expertise in theology, philosophy, social science, church and business administration. The Queen's Foundation has enjoyed the generous co-operation of a number of dioceses, educational institutions and membership organisations within the Church during the course of the project.

LIST OF PUBLICATIONS EMERGING FROM QUEEN'S FOUNDATION AUTHORITY AND GOVERNANCE PROJECT

BOOKS

Noel Timms and Kenneth Wilson editors *Governance and Authority in the Roman Catholic Church: Beginning a Conversation* SPCK, London 2000

Noel Timms editor *Diocesan Dispositions and Parish Voices in the Roman Catholic Church* Matthew James Publishing, Chelmsford 2001

Noel Timms *"You Aren't One of the Boys", Authority in the Catholic Priesthood* Matthew James Publishing, Chelmsford 2001

Andrew Bebb and Anna Roper editors *A Painful Process* Matthew James Publishing, Chelmsford 2001

Joseph A Selling editor *Embracing Sexuality: Authority and Experience in the Catholic Church* Ashgate Publishing, Aldershot 2001

Bernard Hoose editor *Authority in the Roman Catholic Church: Theory and Practice* Ashgate Publishing 2002

Gerard Mannion, Richard Gaillardetz, Jan Kerkhofs and Kenneth Wilson editors *Readings in Church Authority: Gifts and Challenges for Contemporary Catholicism* Ashgate Publishing (forthcoming) 2002

BOOKLETS

Outcaste to Authority Catholic Association for Racial Justice, London 2000

Bernard Hoose *Authority in Roman Catholicism* Matthew James Publishing 2002

David Barker *Change, Communication and Relationships in the Catholic Church* Matthew James Publishing 2002

Annette Barker *Leadership, Formation and Participation in the Parish* Matthew James Publishing (forthcoming)

NOTES

[1] P Verity "Comfort and Challenge" *Priests and People* Volume 15 Number 8,9 August/September 2001

[2] A H Halsey " One Hundred Years of Social Change" *Social Trends 30; 2000 Edition* The Office for National Statistics, London 2000

[3] Men enter the labour force later and leave earlier than in the first half of the century. The percentage of economically active males aged 16-64 years fell from 91% as recently as 1971 to 84% in 1999. In the same period, the percentage of economically active women aged 15-59 years increased from 56% to 72%, favouring education, health and public administration and dominating the expanding clerical and secretarial jobs (employing 18% only of the total workforce in 1901, but, 40% by 1991). Employment in agriculture, textiles, mining and manufacturing declined significantly.

[4] A H Halsey ibid.

[5] A H Halsey ibid.

[6] See J Scott "Family Change: Demographic & Attitudinal Trends Across Nations and Time" *Economic and Social Research Council Research Results* No. 1 June 1997

[7] D Barker "European Values and the Catholic Church" in N Timms and K Wilson (eds.) *Governance and Authority in the Roman Catholic Church,* SPCK London 2000

[8] D Barker, L Halman and A Vloet *The European Values Study 1981-1990; Summary Report* The Gordon Cook Foundation, Aberdeen 1992

[9] *Catholics and their use of Information Sources* NOP Research Group survey for the Catholic Media Trust November 1997, a representative sample involving 5573 interviews.

[10] M P Hornsby-Smith *Roman Catholics in England* Cambridge University Press London 1987.

[11] The 1997 NOP data collected for the Catholic Media Trust directly compares the social class of Catholics with the general population. It is also possible to compare the NOP information on age with national statistics. There are small differences (the age data suggests a slight over representation of Catholics aged 55-64 years), but the broad age bands 15-34; 35-54; and 55 or over are very similar. As far as education is concerned, the NOP data suggest that 31% of Catholics have been educated beyond the age of 16 yrs compared to 27% in the population as a whole.

[12] See M P Hornsby-Smith *Roman Catholics in England* op. cit. and D Ryan *The Catholic Parish* Sheed and Ward London 1996

[13] D Ryan op. cit. p202

[14] M Hornsby-Smith p27

[15] D Barker "Values and Volunteering" in J Davis Smith ed. *Volunteering in Europe: Opportunities and Challenges for the 90's,* Voluntary Action Research, Second Series Paper No.4, The Volunteer Centre Berkhamsted 1993

[16] A Park "The generation game" in Roger Jowell et al editors *British Social Attitudes. 17th Report: Focusing on Diversity,* Sage and the National Centre for Social Research London 2000.

[17] G Davie *Religion in Modern Europe: A Memory Mutates* Oxford University Press Oxford 2000, p96-97

[18] The 1997 NOP Survey for the Catholic Media Trust op. cit.

[19] J Fulton et al *Young Catholics at the Millennium,* University of Dublin Press Dublin 2000

[20] G Davie op. cit. p161

[21] See for example D Gerard "Religious Attitudes and Values" in M Abrams et al editors *Values and Social Change in Britain,* Macmillan, Basingstoke 1985

[22] *Ratio Fundamentalis* subsection 4 quoted in *The Charter for Priestly Formation* Bishops' Conference of England and Wales 1990 and Sacred Congregation for Catholic Education January 1991

[23] See J O'Brien *Seeds of a New Church* The Columbia Press, Blackrock 1994

[24] J M Weiss 'The Council of Trent' in *The New Dictionary of Theology* J A Komonchak, M Collins and D A Lane eds Michael Glazier 1987

[25] E Duffy 'Priests for Ever' *Priests & People* June 1996

[26] N Timms *" You Aren't One of the Boys": Authority in the Catholic Priesthood* Matthew James Chelmsford 2001 an analysis of the results of a National Opinion Poll (NOP) survey of clerical attitudes to authority and governance conducted for the Queen's Foundation project.

[27] N Timms *Diocesan Dispositions and Parish Voices in the Roman Catholic Church* Matthew James Chelmsford 2001

[28] Ryan op. cit.

[29] N Cooper *Collaborative Ministry: Communion, Contention, Commitment.* Paulist Press New York 1993

[30] D McLoughlin "Authority as Service in Communion" in Timms and Wilson (eds.) *Governance and Authority in the Catholic Church* op. cit.

[31] M H Clark "The Pastoral Exercise of Authority" *New Theology Review* August 1997

[32] E Duffy "Papal Authority" and R Markus "Recovering the Ancient Tradition" in *Priests & People* Vol.11 Numbers 8, 9. 1997. The Tablet, London

[33] W Kaspar "On the Church: A Friendly reply to Cardinal Ratzinger" *America* 23-30th April 2001

[34] J R Quinn *The Reform of the Papacy: the Costly Call to Unity* Crossroads, New York 1999

[35] B Hoose *Authority in Roman Catholicism* Matthew James 2001

[36] P Grindell "Diocesan Structures and Resources" in N Timms ed. *Diocesan Dispositions and Parish Voices* op. cit.

[37] Anna Rowland *"Reflections on the Lay Ministry of Women in the Catholic Church",* report for the Margaret Beaufort Institute, Cambridge, presented at the Queen's Foundation Conference on Authority and Governance in the Catholic Church, Robinson College, Cambridge June 2000

[38] L Fitzgerald "Seeking Extended Dialogue: Change and Development in the Roman Catholic Church" in Noel Timms ed. *Diocesan Dispositions and Parish Voices* op. cit.

[39] M H Hornsby-Smith "Findings From the Parishes" in N Timms ed. *Diocesan Dispositions and Parish Voices* op. cit.

[40] M P Hornsby-Smith *Roman Catholics in England* reports that "close involvement with the institutional Church was also associated with a strong attachment to the traditional norms of the Catholic Church" including doctrinal orthodoxy, sexual morality, marriage and religious practice. The European Values surveys suggested a similar finding, see D Gerard in *Values and Social Change in Britain* eds. M Abrams, D Gerard and N Timms, Macmillan London 1985

[41] K Kelly "Some Theological Reflections" in *Diocesan Dispositions and Parish Voices* op. cit.

[42] C Barbour "The pastoral needs of the laity" in *Priests and People* Volume 15 Number 8,9 August/ September 2001

[43] Annette Barker *Leadership, Formation and Participation in the Parish,* Matthew James, Chelmsford, 2001

[44] S Lindsell "How do we care for the carers?" *Priests and People* Volume 15 Number 8,9 August/September 2001

[45] Testimony supplied by Fr. John Clark in *Personal Testimonies of Experience of Authority and Governance in the Church,* prepared for the Queen's Foundation Conference on Authority and Governance, Darwen, Lancashire, November 1997

[46] K Kelly "Some Theological Reflections" op. cit.

[47] J Armitage " The vocation of pastoral work", *Priests and People* Volume 15 8,9 August/September 2001

[48] Kevin Kelly "Some Theological Reflections" op. cit.

[49] G Soares Prabhu *The Kingdom of God: Jesus' Vision of a New Society* National Biblical Catechetical Centre, Bangalore 1981. See also W McConville 'Mission' in J A Komonchak et al (eds) *The New Dictionary of Theology,* op. cit.

[50] Kevin Kelly "Some Theological Reflections" op. cit.

[51] D Barker " Values and Volunteering" in Justin Smith ed. *Volunteering in Europe* op. cit.

[52] Quoted in D Barker et al. *The European Values Survey* op. cit.

[53] Revelations 3:15-16

[54] P Murnion "pastoral care in US parishes" *Priests and People* Volume 15 Number 8,9 August/September 2001

[55] The reference to *"the sudden theological changes"* which took place as priests moved in and out of the parish refers to the different, and sometimes conflicting, theological perspectives of the priests themselves, not to changes introduced by the Church authorities. These differences affected relationships and meant additional pressure upon the parish community in a time of crisis.

[56] Fr. Kevin Kelly "Some Theological Reflections" p171 op. cit.

[57] At the presentation of results of the various studies held at Queen's College, Birmingham March 2001

[58] J Mahoney sj " Theological and Pastoral Reflections" in M. Abrams, D. Gerard and N. Timms eds *Values and Social Change in Britain"* op. cit.

[59] E Schillebeeckx "Church: The Human Face of God" SCM London 1990 p219, quoted in K Kelly "Some Theological Reflections" op. cit